Changes

Contents

Teachers' notes

The aims of this book

▲ To introduce the notion of change in the world around us.
▲ To promote awareness of physical and chemical changes, both in the natural world and in human activities.
▲ To provide experience in observing, predicting, recording, measuring and making hypotheses.
▲ To provide opportunities for children to share their ideas with others.

Developing science skills

While it is not necessary to follow the order of the worksheets, it is important that all those covering one aspect of the subject, such as the weather, are dealt with at approximately the same time.

Although it is in the doing of science that children learn best, this involves more than just practical work. They need to observe, record, predict, measure, look for patterns, classify, explain and ask questions that can lead to further investigations. They need time to discuss their work, before and after the activity; this will also aid the teacher in monitoring the children's progress so that they build a valid framework for future development.

Safety precautions

All the activities described in this book use everyday equipment and materials which are perfectly safe if used sensibly. If extra care is needed on some activities, this is mentioned in the body of the worksheet and again in these notes.

Scientific background

Scientific background information has been provided in the teachers' notes to help you understand the scientific concepts and ideas covered. It generally goes beyond the level of understanding of most children, but will give you the confidence to ask and answer questions and guide the children in their investigations.

Page 5: Solids, liquids and gases

Key idea: To introduce the terms *solid, liquid* and *gas*.
Scientific background: The molecules in solids stay in one position, hence solids can maintain a definite shape. The molecules in a liquid stay close together, but move about. The molecules in a gas move about very rapidly and rebound from one another.
Likely outcome: butter – solid; honey – liquid; wood – solid; bubbles – gas; inside a balloon – gas; salt – solid; ice lolly – solid; candle – solid; ketchup – liquid; paper – solid; steam – gas; nail – solid.

Page 6: Changing solids, liquids and gases

Key idea: To investigate the changes of matter.
Scientific background: Applying heat causes molecules to move faster, hence a solid can be turned into a liquid and liquid into a gas. Vinegar (an acid) will react with baking powder to form carbon dioxide.
Likely outcome: Water boiled turns to steam (gas), fruit juice frozen turns to ice (solid), baking powder and vinegar form carbon dioxide (gas), butter heated melts (liquid), sugar dissolves in hot water (liquid).
Safety precaution: Ensure the kettle lead is out of reach. Do not let children use boiling water unsupervised.

Extension: Investigate other changes of state – do all solids melt? Can all liquids freeze? and so on.

Page 7: Separating substances

Key idea: How filters can clean water.
Scientific background: Filtration involves the use of a barrier to hold back particles of solids. Groundwater is filtered as it passes through layers of rocks and soil. The solution passing through the filter is called the filtrate, insoluble material on the filter is the residue.
Likely outcome: The muddy water will become clear as it filters through. Finer filters are more effective.
Extension: Filter a variety of waters, e.g. tap, pond, river, mineral, to find out which is the cleanest.

Page 8: Dissolving things

Key idea: Dissolving substances in water.
Scientific background: Not all substances dissolve in water and some only partially dissolve. Heating increases the rate of dissolving. Fine powders dissolve more quickly than coarse ones. Water is called the solvent and the substance dissolved is called the solute. Solvent + solute = solution.
Likely outcome: Sugar and salt will dissolve; pepper flour and scouring powder will not dissolve; bicarbonate of soda will partially dissolve.
Extension: Investigate other solvents, e.g. turpentine will dissolve fats and oils that will not dissolve in water.

Page 9: Physical and chemical changes

Key idea: To differentiate between physical and chemical changes.
Scientific background: In a physical change no new substance is formed or destroyed, there is no change in weight, it can usually be reversed easily and the energy changes are usually small. In chemical changes, the substance is changed and new substances are formed, there is a change in weight, a reverse change is difficult and the energy changes are often large.
Likely outcome: The ice lolly, wood, drink can and heated milk undergo a physical change, while the yoghurt and bread are the result of chemical changes.

Page 10: Making chemical changes

Key idea: Chemical changes in substances.
Scientific background: Steel is mostly iron. Iron combines with oxygen in the air to form iron oxide (rust). Water helps to speed up the chemical action. As wood burns, water, carbon dioxide, methane, pentane, hexane and octane are produced.
Likely outcome: The steel wool will rust, the matchstick turns to charcoal and the paper to ash.

Page 11: Manufactured changes

Key idea: To differentiate between a raw material and a manufactured material.
Likely outcome: Raw materials – diamond, oil, iron ore, gold, wool, coal, salt, milk and silk. Glass, steel, plastic, flour, aluminium and petrol are manufactured.
Extension: Make a list of raw and manufactured materials in the classroom. Find out where the raw materials come from in the world and how they are made into manufactured products.

Page 12: Changing colours

Key ideas: Mixing primary colours and mixing shades of colour. To mix colours through spinning.
Scientific background: Different (secondary) colours can be made using the three primary colours – red, yellow and blue. White light is made up of all the colours of the rainbow. We see an object as being a certain colour because that colour is reflected by the object. In a spinning disc, your eyes are deceived because they cannot pick out the separate colours. If the disc was painted the seven colours of the rainbow, it would look white when spun.
Likely outcome: blue and yellow – green; red and yellow – orange; red and blue – purple; red, blue and yellow – dirty brown; blue and white – light blue; red and white – pink; yellow and white – light yellow, cream.

Page 13: Chromatography

Key idea: How one colour is made up of different colours.
Scientific background: Some colours will quickly spread out, others will move slowly.
Extension: Try different water temperatures.

Page 14: Changing sounds

Key idea: Changing musical sounds.
Scientific background: Sound is caused by vibrations. Blowing across the top of a bottle causes the air inside the bottle to vibrate. Differences in pitch are caused by the amount of water inside and the type of bottle used (less mass of air = higher pitch).
Likely outcome: Different amounts of water, different lengths and thicknesses of rubber bands and differing amounts and types of beads inside a container will produce different sounds.
Extension: Make a class band with hitting, shaking, plucking, beating and blowing instruments.

Page 15: Changes in strength

Key idea: How to make paper stronger.
Likely outcome: Paper which is folded or rolled will be much stronger than flat paper.
Extension: Make a bridge from newspaper which will stand and has the longest span.

Page 16: Animal life cycles

Key idea: To observe the stages in life cycles.
Extension: Find out about more difficult insects such as butterflies.
Note: Check with the LEA about keeping animals in classrooms; some do not allow tadpoles to be taken from ponds. Mealworms are excellent for observing all stages of the life cycle at once. They can be obtained from pet shops and are easy to maintain.

Page 17: How plants change

Key idea: The various stages of growth of a bean plant.
Likely outcome: Bean seed, seed with small root, seed with long root and small shoot, longer roots and shoot, tall plant, tall plant with flowers, tall plant with some flowers dead and a few small bean pods, tall plant with most flowers dead and more bean pods, tall plant with large bean pods.
Extension: Grow bean seeds under different conditions such as in shade, in the dark, with water, without water, in soil, in sand.

Page 18: Photosynthesis

Key idea: How photosynthesis works.
Likely outcome: The covered leaves will be lighter in colour than the other leaves. The amount of photosynthesis depends on the amount of light energy received. When testing for starch, the part of the leaf exposed to light becomes coloured by the iodine due to the presence of starch. Bubbles of oxygen are produced by the pondweed when in sunlight, less bubbles are produced when in the dark.

Page 19: Will it rot?

Key idea: To investigate food decay, mould growth.
Safety precautions: Do not open the bags once they are prepared as spores from mould are harmful.
Likely outcome: Food which is damp, warm or dirty (wiped on the floor) will go mouldy more quickly.
Extension: Discuss safe food handling and hygiene.

Page 20: Making compost

Key idea: To have firsthand experience of making compost; to investigate the use of compost.
Scientific background: Decay occurs due to decomposers such as bacteria, fungi and earthworms. The processes involved produce heat and the compost can steam. The smell produced by rotting food is caused by the nitrogen- and sulphur-compounds formed.
Likely outcome: The compost becomes dark and crumbly. The seed planted in compost will grow better than the other.
Extension: Find out about other recycling/reusing processes and environmental issues.

Page 21: Genetics

Key idea: Certain characteristics are inherited.
Scientific background: We inherit genes for certain traits from one parent and genes for other traits from the other parent. Some traits are dominant and others are recessive and this determines which parental trait is inherited.
Likely outcome: Eyes – dark/hazel and green are dominant; hair – dark is dominant; freckles are dominant; ear lobes – free is dominant; nose – turned up is dominant. Be aware of children who may not know their real parents.
Extension: Explore evolutionary changes from dinosaurs to modern-day creatures.

Page 22: Fossils

Key idea: To illustrate how fossils are formed.
Extension: Visit places where fossils are found. Make a 'dig' in the school grounds. Find out how fossils tell us how creatures have changed over time.

Page 23: Changes in the landscape

Key idea: To provide opportunities to discuss the effects humans have on the landscape.
Likely outcome: 1 positive: jobs created, better transport; negative: pollution from factories and cars, wildlife habitats destroyed, farm land decreased. 2 positive: wildlife habitats created, pollution cleaned up, recreation place created. 3 positive: more homes provided, jobs created; negative: farming land destroyed, pollution from waste, cars and so on.
Extension: Discuss the environmental impact of humans – ozone layer, greenhouse effect, pollution.

Page 24: Human life cycle

Key idea: To provide a discussion point for understanding the stages of the human life cycle.
Likely outcomes: 1 feeds itself, toilet trained, walks, begins to talk; 2 goes to school, reads and writes, plays sports, talks well, friendships develop, grows, puberty; 3 starts work, more permanent relationships, body strong and supple; 4 loss of hair or greying, stooping, wrinkles.
Extension: Make a human life cycle collage. Compare life cycles to those of other animals and plants.

Page 25: Changing speed

Key idea: To introduce the notion that friction is a force which slows moving objects.
Likely outcome: The heavier car creates more friction and moves more slowly, making it travel less distance. Objects of lesser mass accelerate at a greater rate. Cars move more quickly on smooth wood than on rough wood which creates more friction.
Extension: Find out if heavier objects fall more quickly than lighter objects.

Page 26: The water cycle

Key idea: To introduce the concept of the water cycle and how water is used by humans.
Likely outcome: 1 – evaporation, 2 – water vapour, 3 – condensation, 4 – precipitation, 5 – runoff, 6 – groundwater, 7 – irrigation, 8 – purification, 9 – evaporation.
Extension: Demonstrate how rain is made by boiling a kettle and holding a tray of ice above the steam. Water will condense and drops of 'rain' will fall.

Page 27: Changes in the weather – temperature

Key idea: To investigate changes in air temperature.
Likely outcome: The air temperature will be cooler in the shade and warmer at the middle of the day.
Extension: Investigate the 'chill factor', placing some thermometers in the wind and some out of the wind.

Page 28: Changing direction

Key idea: Changing the shape and weight of a paper aeroplane can alter the direction in which it flies.
Likely outcome: Flap up on right: plane goes right; flap up on left: plane goes left; both flaps up: plane goes up; both flaps down: plane goes down; clip on nose: plane nose dives; clip on tail: plane lands tail first.
Extension: Do different designs affect flight?

Page 29: Shadows

Key idea: To observe how shadows change length and position throughout the day.
Likely outcome: The shortest shadow is in the middle of the day, which may not be exactly at noon.
Extension: Does the shadow change direction at different times? What happens over several weeks?

Page 30: The seasons

Key idea: How the seasons affects plants and animals.
Likely outcome: Hedgehog hibernates, beech loses leaves. Holly produces berries, stoats' fur turns white. Swallows return, daffodil flowers. Grass grows quickly, salmon migrate to spawn.
Extension: Look at other plants and animals.

Page 31: Day and night

Key idea: The changes which occur to the environment during the day and night.
Likely outcome: The hours of daylight will depend on the season – more in summer than in winter.
Extension: Demonstrate how night and day are created using a lamp and a globe.

Page 32: Changes in the moon

Key idea: Why the moon changes shape.
Likely outcome:

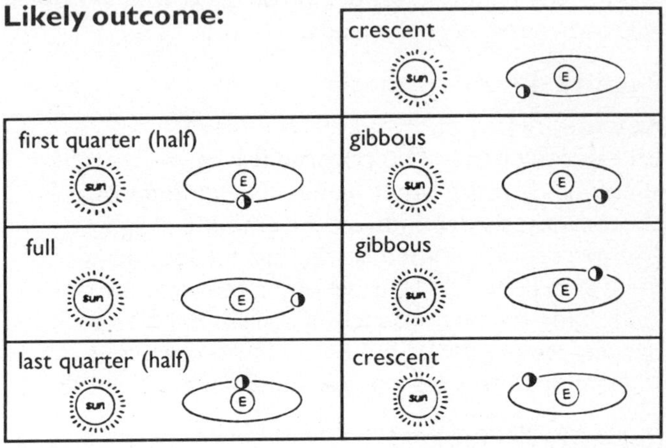

	crescent sun E
first quarter (half) sun E	gibbous sun E
full sun E	gibbous sun E
last quarter (half) sun E	crescent sun E

National Curriculum: Science

In addition to Experimental and investigative science, the following PoS of the National Curriculum for science are relevant to this book:

Life processes and living things
Pupils should be taught:
- ▲ that there are life processes common to all animals;
- ▲ that plant growth is affected by availability of light and water and by temperature;
- ▲ that green plants make food using energy from the Sun;
- ▲ the life cycle of plants, including pollination, germination and seed dispersal;
- ▲ that different plants and animals are found in different habitats;
- ▲ how different animals and plants in two different habitats are suited to their environment.

Materials and their properties
Pupils should be taught:
- ▲ to compare everyday materials on the basis of properties such as strength;
- ▲ that materials come from a range of sources;
- ▲ to recognise differences between solids, liquids and gases;
- ▲ that solid particles of different sizes can be separated by sieving;
- ▲ that some solids dissolve in liquids to give solutions but some do not;
- ▲ that insoluble solids can be separated from solutions by filtering;
- ▲ that solids that have dissolved can be recovered by evaporating the liquid from the solution;
- ▲ that mixing, heating or cooling materials can cause them to change;
- ▲ the part that evaporation and condensation play in the water cycle;
- ▲ to consider what process caused a change.

Physical processes
Pupils should be taught :
- ▲ that temperature is a measure of how hot things are;
- ▲ that sounds are made when objects vibrate;
- ▲ that the pitch and loudness of sounds depend on the way in which the object vibrates;
- ▲ that we see things when light scattered from them enters our eyes;
- ▲ that the Earth orbits the Sun;
- ▲ that the planets orbit the Sun and that the Moon orbits the Earth;
- ▲ that the Earth spins around its own axis;
- ▲ how day and night are related to the spin of the Earth.

see inside back cover for Scottish and Northern Ireland curriculum links

▲ Name ______________________________

Solids, liquids and gases

A **solid** is something which usually does not change its shape, for example, a rock, sugar.
A **liquid** is something which can flow from one place to another, for example, water, milk.
A **gas** cannot usually be seen. It fills the whole space it is in, for example, the air around us.

▲ Look at the objects below. Decide whether each is a solid, liquid or gas.

▲ Make a list of the solids, liquids and gases in your classroom. Share your list with others. Do they agree?

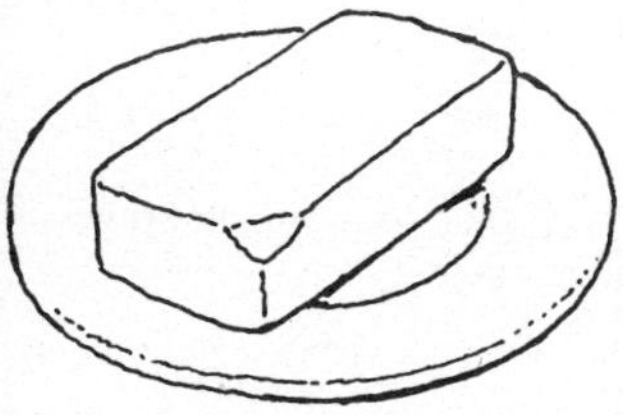 butter	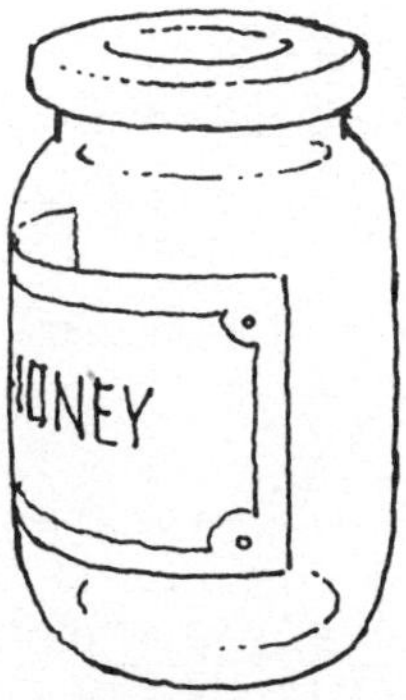 honey	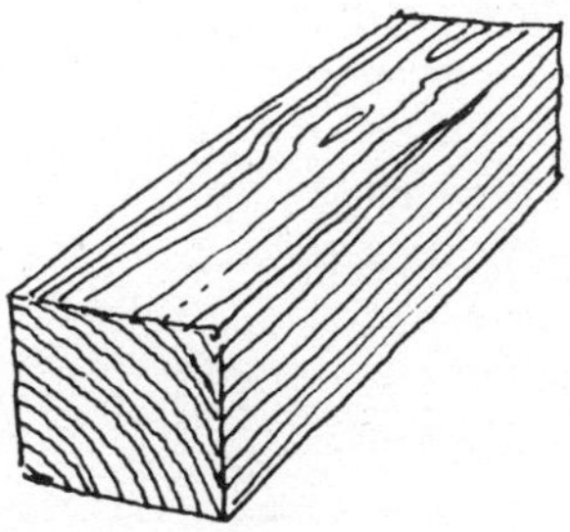 wood	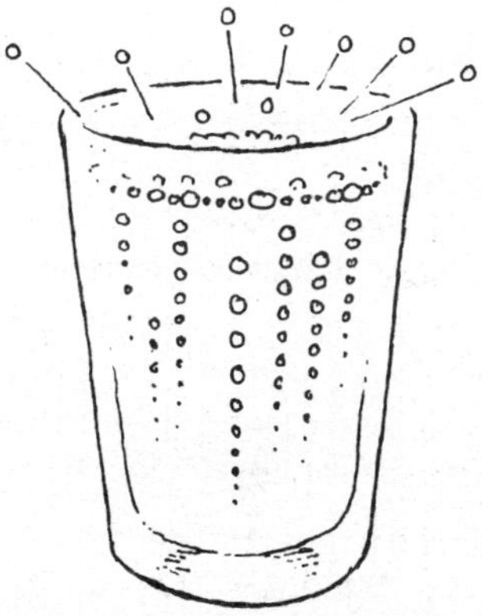 bubbles in soft drink
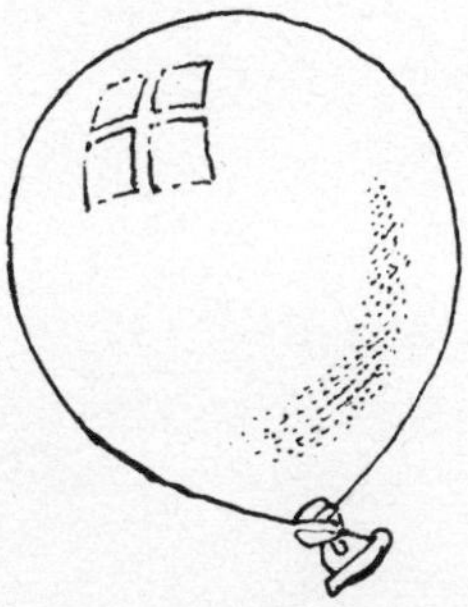 inside a balloon	 salt	 ice lolly	 candle
 ketchup	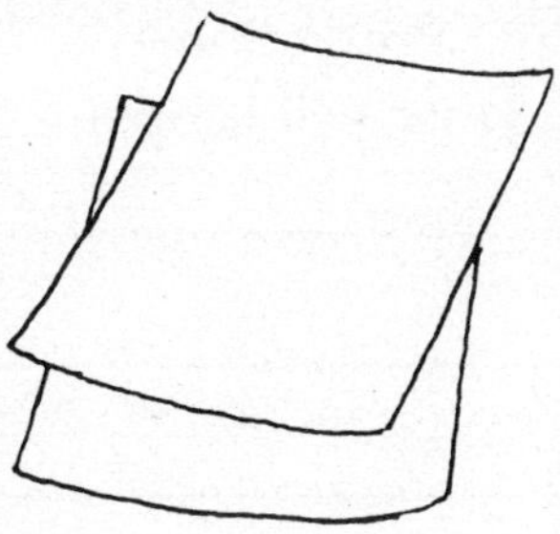 paper	 steam	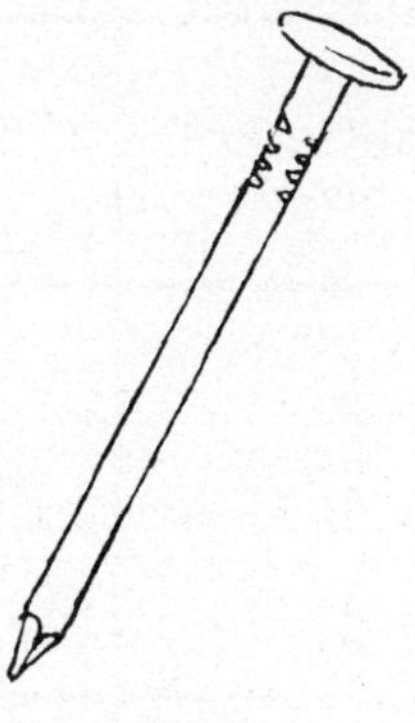 nail

▲ Name ______________________________

Changing solids, liquids and gases

You will need: water; kettle; ice-tray; fruit juice; butter; saucepan; hotplate; baking powder; vinegar; sugar; jars; spoon; fridge; cup.

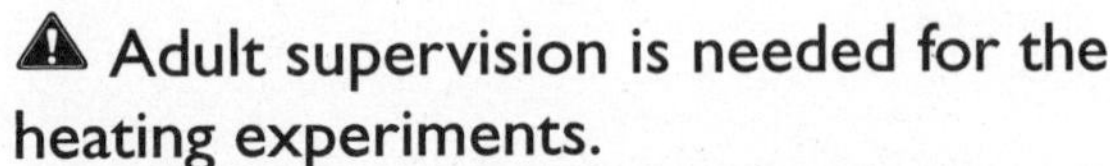

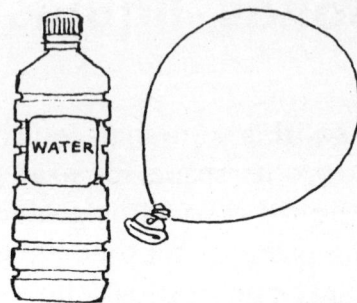

⚠ Adult supervision is needed for the heating experiments.

1 Boil some water. What happens?

2 Put some fruit juice in the freezer compartment of a fridge. Leave for several hours.

3 Put a teaspoon of baking powder into a jar. Add vinegar.

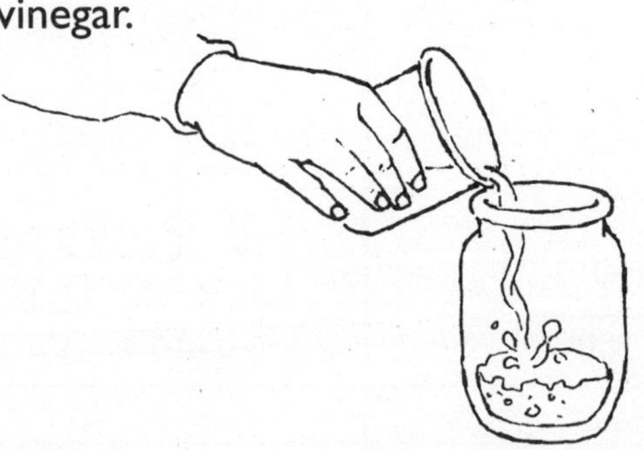

4 Heat some butter in a saucepan.

5 Boil some water. Add it to a cup with a teaspoon of sugar in it. Stir.

▲ Record your findings here.

Experiment	Substance	Action	Prediction – what will happen?	Result – what did it change to? solid? liquid? gas?
1	water	boil it		
2	fruit juice	freeze it		
3	baking powder	add vinegar		
4	butter	heat it		
5	sugar	add hot water		

▲ Name ______________________

Separating substances

You will need: salt; water; glass; spoon; saucepan; hotplate.

Some things are made from two or more substances. Sometimes it is necessary to separate them in order to obtain one of the substances. We can do this by evaporation and filtering.

▲ Try this for yourself.
⚠ Adult supervision is needed.

1 Mix several teaspoons of salt in a glass of water until the salt dissolves.

2 Pour the solution into a saucepan and boil the water.

3 Observe what happens to the water. Where does it go? What is left over after the water has gone?

▲ Filtering
1 Set up a filter as in the diagram.
2 Fill the top with muddy water.
3 Watch the water which comes out. How has it changed?

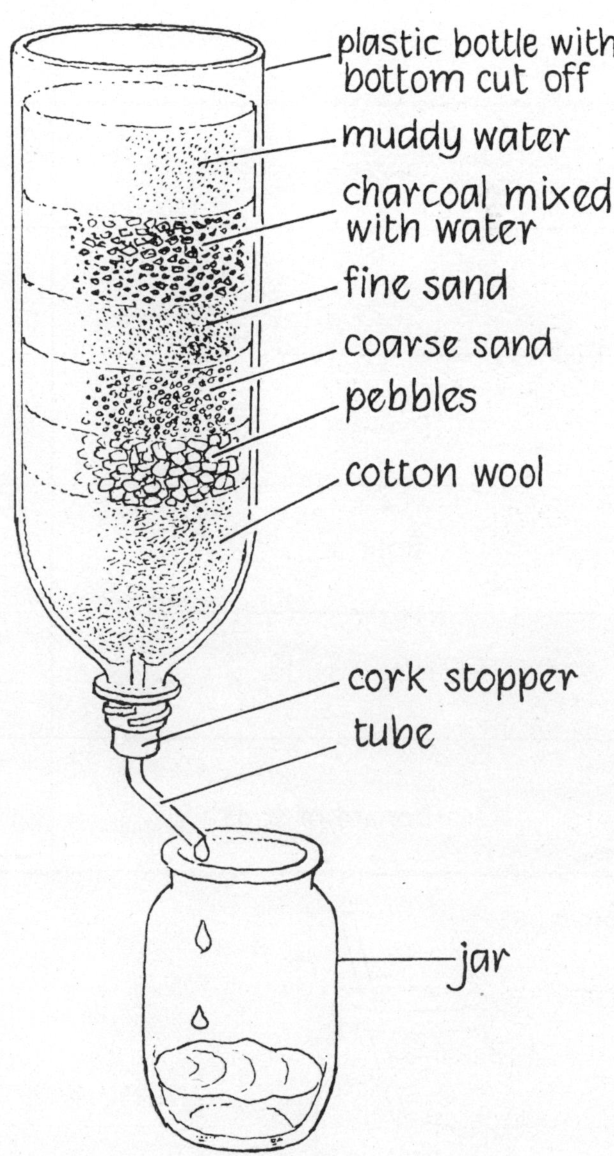

▲ Try out simpler filters such as paper, tights, socks, fabric. Which filter works best?

▲ Name ______________________

Dissolving things

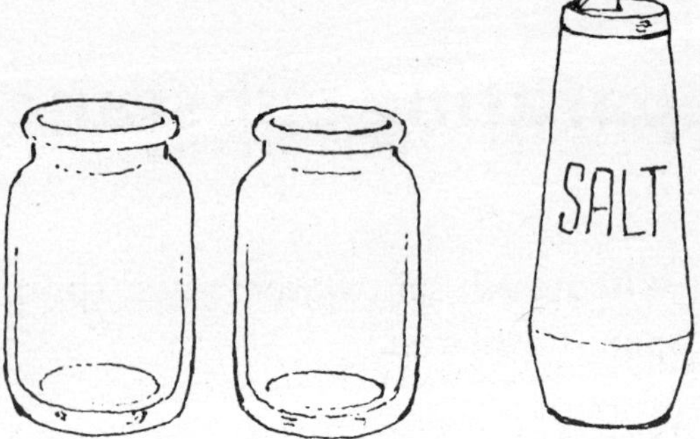

You will need: jam jars; water; sugar; salt; pepper; flour; scouring powder; bicarbonate of soda; spoon.

1 Fill a jar with water.
2 Add one spoonful of salt.
3 Stir.
4 Does the salt dissolve?

▲ Try out the other ingredients. Predict the result first then record what happens.

▲ Does the water change colour?

Substance	Prediction – will it dissolve?	Result
sugar		
salt		
pepper		
flour		
scouring powder		
bicarbonate of soda		

▲ What affects whether something dissolves or not?
▲ Do fine substances dissolve better than coarse ones? Try different types of sugar.
▲ Does it help to stir the water?
▲ Will heating the water affect how things dissolve?
▲ Which substance dissolves the fastest? Why do you think this is?

▲ Name ______________________________

Physical and chemical changes

When we change the appearance of something without turning it into something else we are making a *physical change*, such as bending a nail or freezing water to make ice.

When we change something into something else we are making a *chemical change*, such as burning wood to make charcoal or smelting iron to make steel.

▲ Look at the following changes. Decide if there has been a physical or chemical change made. Discuss your decision with others. Do they agree?

▲ Make a list of physical and chemical changes which can be made at home or at school.

▲ Name ___________________________

Making chemical changes

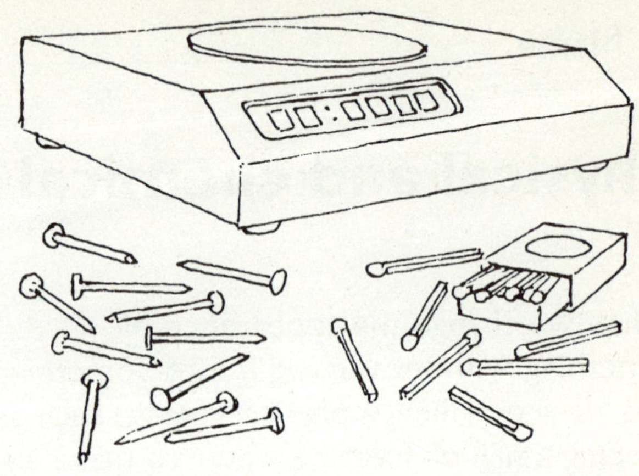

You will need: steel wool; saucer; water; nails; matches; saucer; paper; electronic scales.

Activity 1

▲ Soak some of the steel wool in water then place it on a saucer. Leave for several hours or overnight.

▲ What has happened to the steel wool? Can you suggest why this has happened?

▲ Compare this wool to the wool not placed in the water. Which is strongest?

▲ Try the same experiment with a nail. Think of ways to prevent the nail from rusting. Try out your ideas. Record the results.

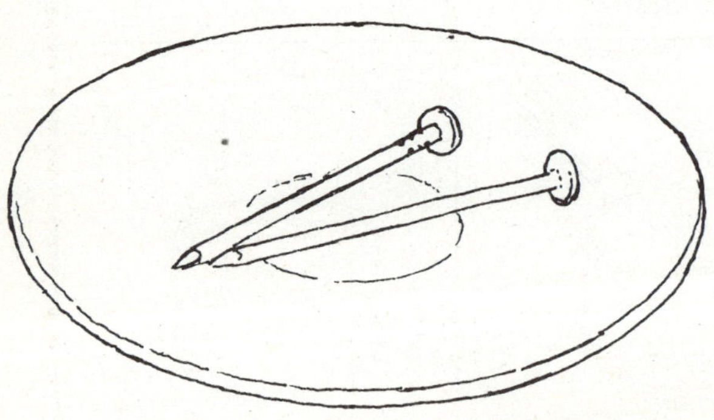

Activity 2

▲ Place a lighted match in a saucer and watch it burn. When cool, touch the match.

▲ What has happened to it? How has it changed?

▲ Cut a small piece of paper and place this into the saucer. Light it with a match. Watch what happens. How has it changed?

▲ Repeat these two experiments but weigh each object before and after. What do you notice?

▲ Name ______________________

Manufactured changes

Humans are able to take a raw material found in nature, such as wood, and change it into something completely different. Wood can be manufactured into paper.

▲ Below is a group of things. For each object decide if it is a raw material or whether it has been changed (manufactured) in some way. Write your answer underneath each picture. You may need to discuss your ideas with a friend or use reference books to help you.

glass	diamond	oil	steel	iron ore
gold	plastic	wool	flour	aluminium
coal	salt	milk	petrol	silk

▲ Name ______________________________

Changing colours

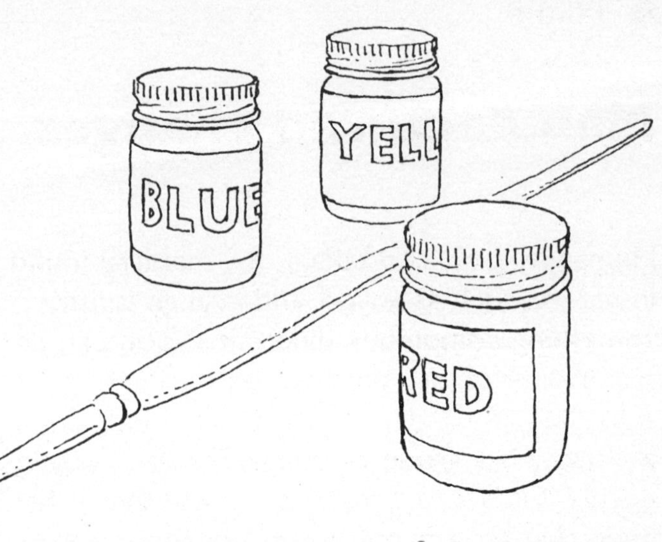

You will need: red, blue, yellow and white paint (or cellophane); paper; paint brush; card; felt-tipped pens; matchstick.

You can make different colours using two or three other colours mixed together.

▲ Try out these mixes:

Colour mix	Prediction – what colour will it make?	Result – what colour did it make?
blue and yellow		
red and yellow		
red and blue		
red, blue and yellow		
blue and white		
red and white		
yellow and white		

▲ How many different shades of each colour can you make?

▲ Can you make black?

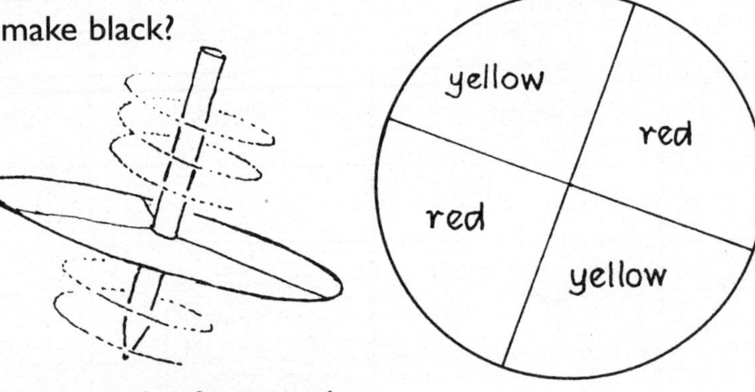

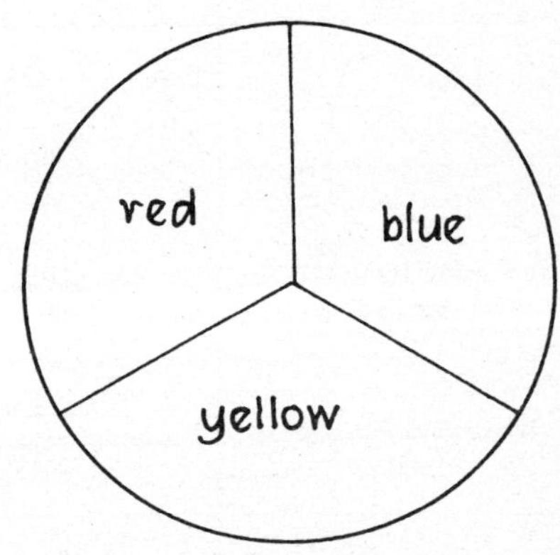

1 Now cut some circles from card.
2 Colour as shown with felt-tipped pens.
3 Make a hole in the centre for a matchstick.
4 Spin the cards quickly. What happens?

▲ Try different colours and patterns. Record the results.

▲ Name ______________________________

Chromatography

You will need: water-based felt-tipped pens; water; jars; blotting paper; food colouring; eye dropper; saucer.

Colours can be changed by mixing with other colours. Chromatography is a method used to separate all the colours which have been mixed together to make one colour.

Activity 1

1 Cut out a square of blotting paper (10cm x 10cm).
2 Draw a circle of any colour felt-tipped pen (or food colouring).
3 Place the paper over a saucer.
4 With an eye dropper, put one drop of water in the centre of the coloured dot.

5 Wait until the ink stops spreading. Add another drop.
6 Repeat.
▲ What happens?

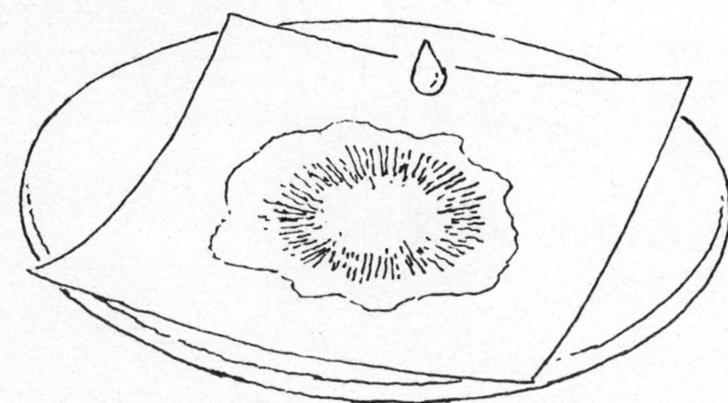

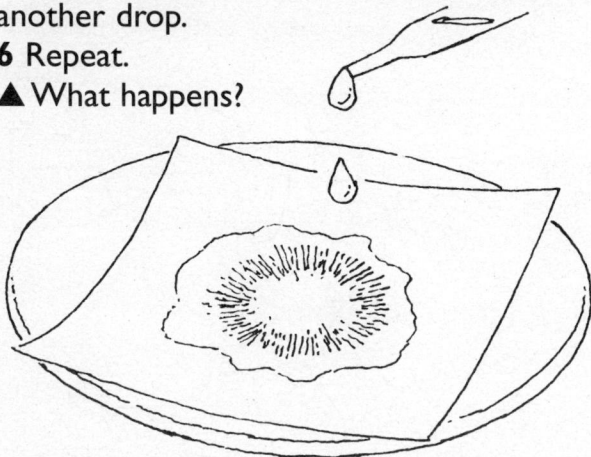

▲ Try out other colours and compare the results.

Activity 2

1 Cut out strips of blotting paper (33cm x 12 cm).
2 Place a dot of colour about 2cm from one end.

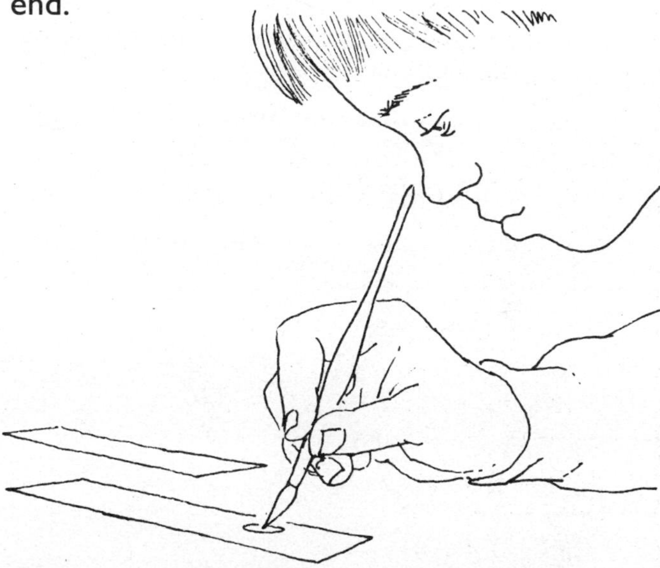

3 Put the strips into a jar of water so the dot of colour is just above the water line.
4 Watch what happens.
▲ Which colour uses the most mixtures?

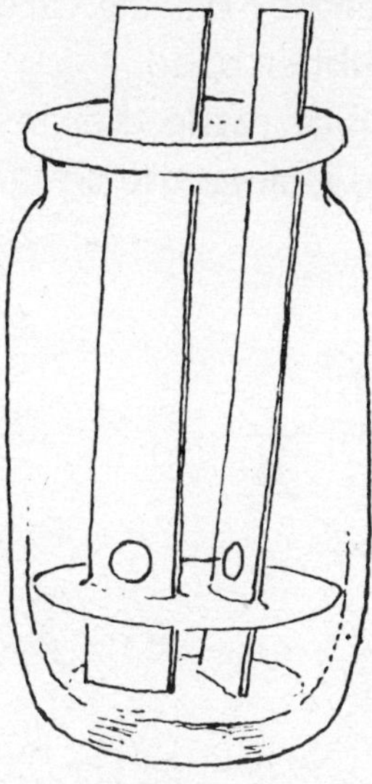

▲ Try out several different brands of the same colour, say, black. Do they all use the same colours to make black?

▲ Name ____________________

Changing sounds

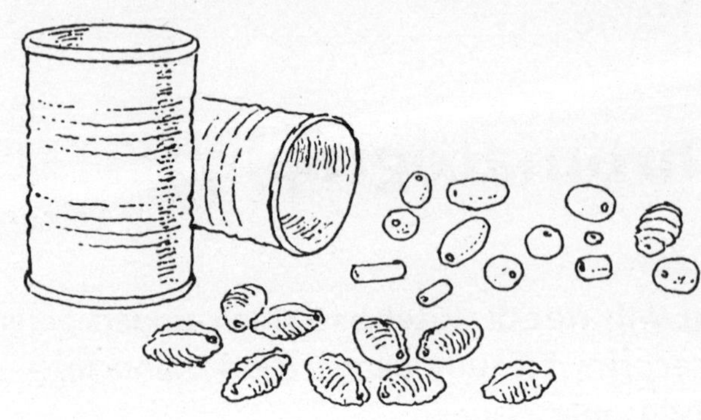

You will need: empty bottles; water; ice-cream cartons; rubber bands; tins; beads; pasta.

Sound is made when objects vibrate. We can change the pitch and loudness of the sound by altering the object making the sound. Pitch refers to how high or low the sound is.

▲ Find out more about pitch and loudness by making some musical instruments.
1 Fill bottles with different amounts of water.
2 Blow across the top of each bottle.
▲ How can you make the sounds higher/lower/louder?

3 Fill tins with objects such as beads and pasta. Seal the end by placing card over it and secure with a rubber band.
4 Hit, shake, roll or rattle the tins.
▲ How can you change the sounds?

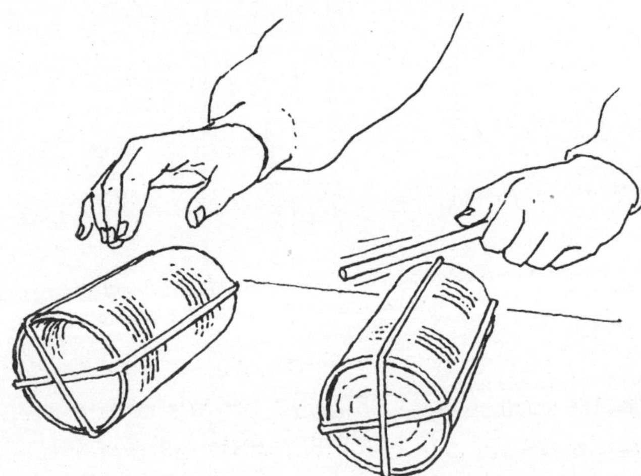

5 Cut slits in the sides of an ice-cream carton at the top. Attach rubber bands and pluck these to make sounds.

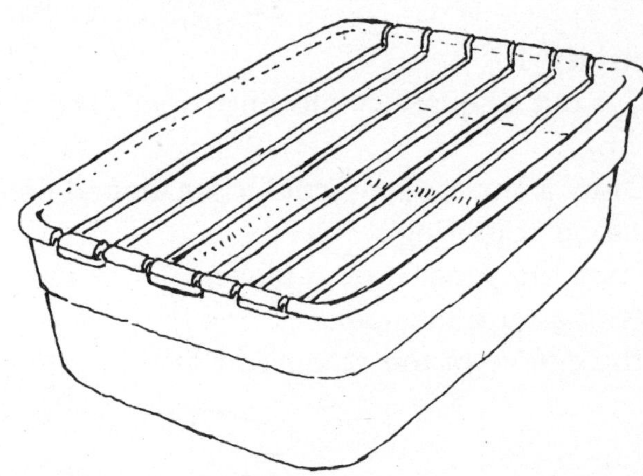

▲ How can you change the sounds? Try different sorts of rubber bands. Does it make a difference if the bands are raised by card?
▲ Can you make an instrument with bands of different lengths? How does this change the sounds made?

▲ Name ______________________________

Changes in strength

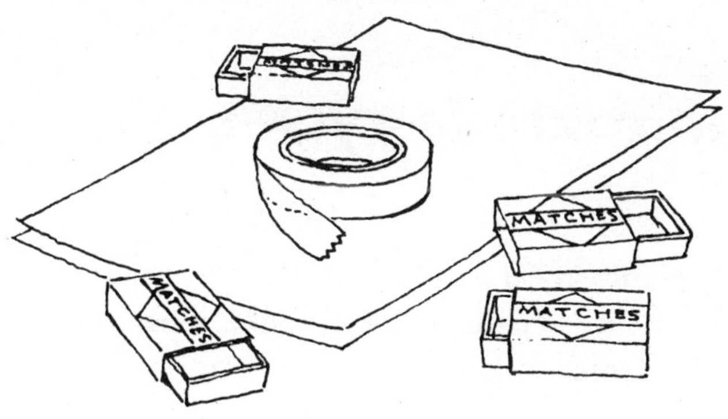

You will need: paper or thin card (A4 size); 4 matchboxes or blocks; measuring weights (1g – 1kg); sticky tape.

We can sometimes change the strength of something by altering its shape.

▲ Conduct this experiment to find out how the strength of paper can be changed.

▲ Use the paper in the following ways. See how much weight the paper will hold each time.

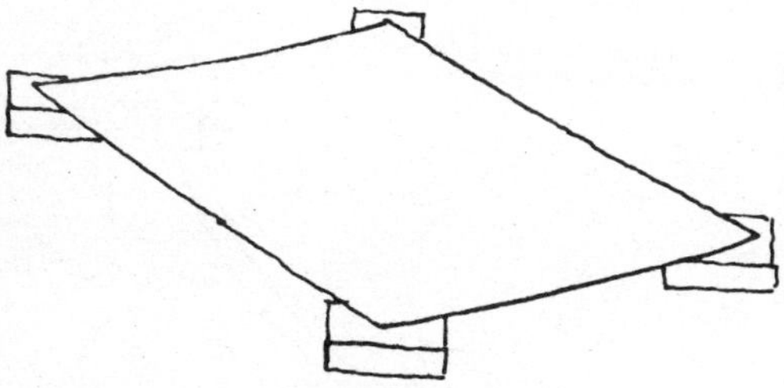

flat

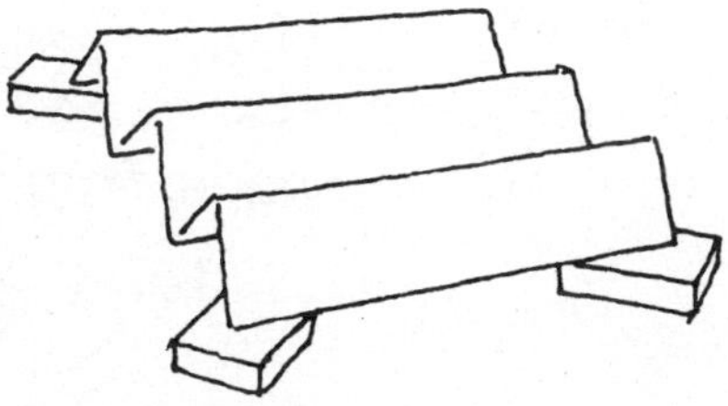

corrugated (triangular)

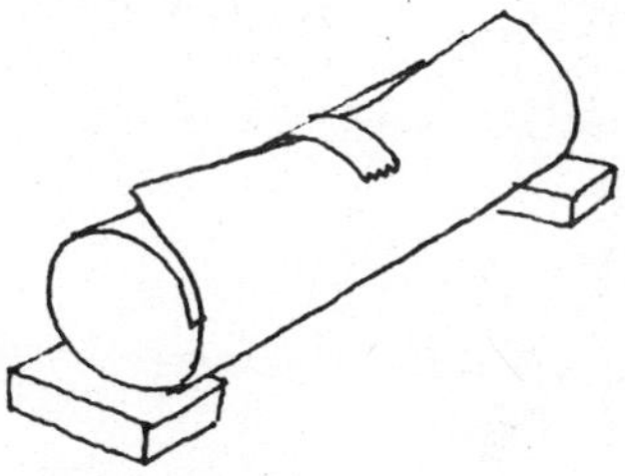

loosely rolled

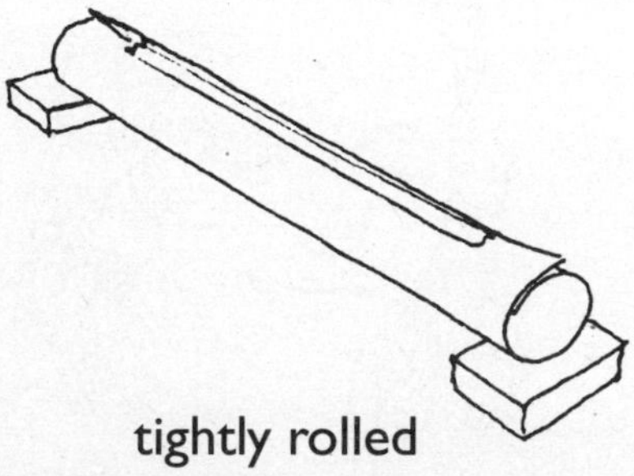

tightly rolled

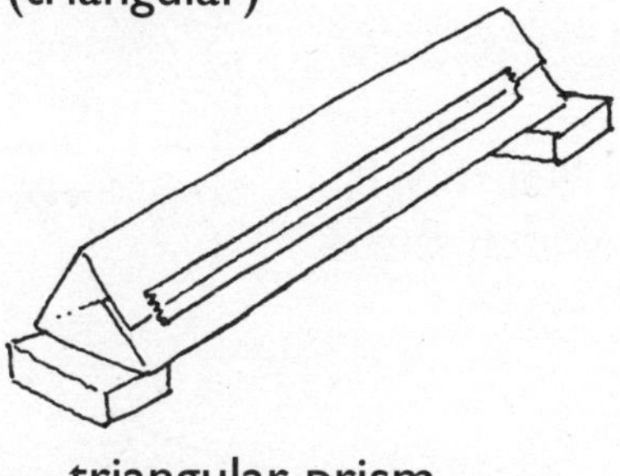

triangular prism

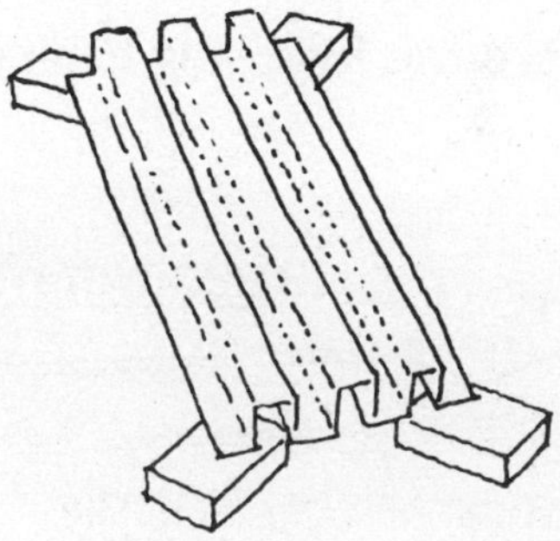

corrugated (rectangular)

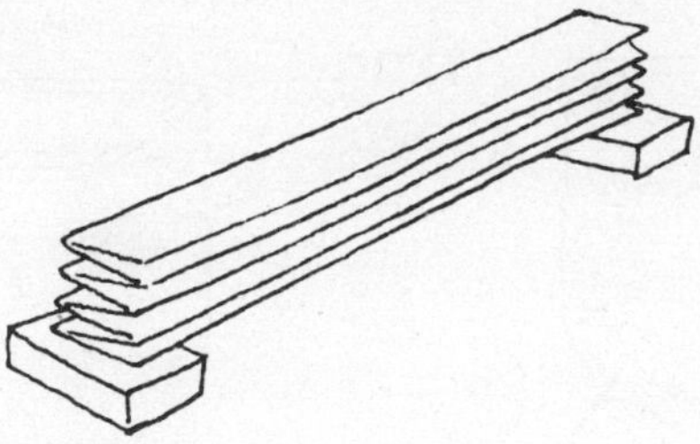

folded flat (ruler width)

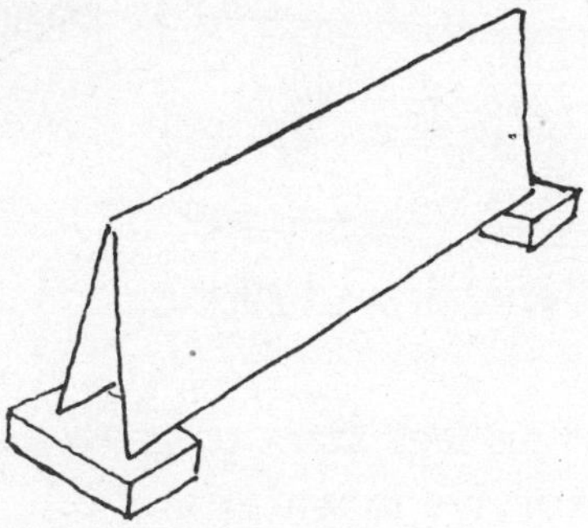

folded in half

▲ Which shape is the strongest? Can you suggest why?

▲ Try out other shapes of your own. Record the results.

▲ How would these shapes affect how buildings or bridges are made?

▲ Name ______________________________

Animal life cycles

Some animals change completely as they grow. Many insects, such as butterflies and mealworms, do this. Frogs do too.

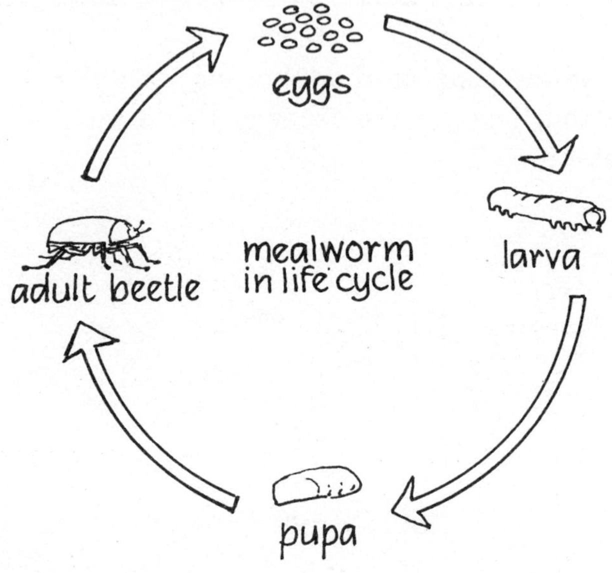

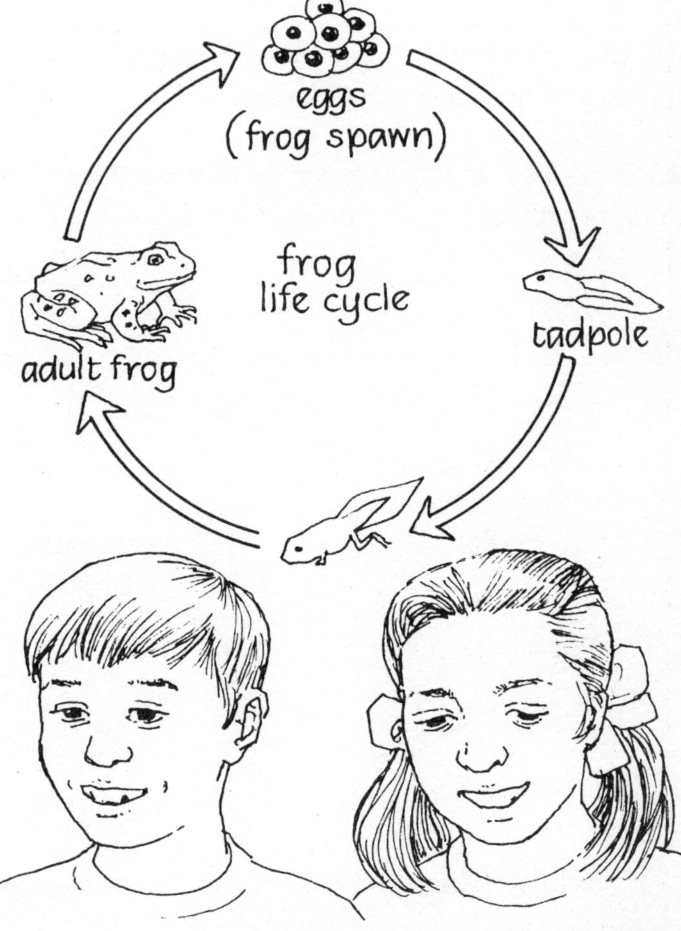

When animals change completely like this, it is called metamorphosis. You can watch these changes yourself.

▲ Prepare the following habitats:

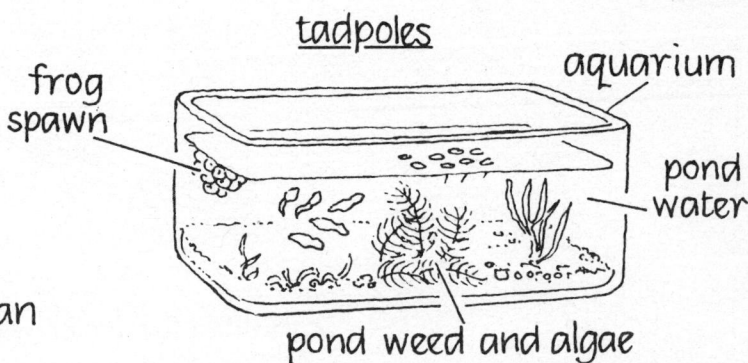

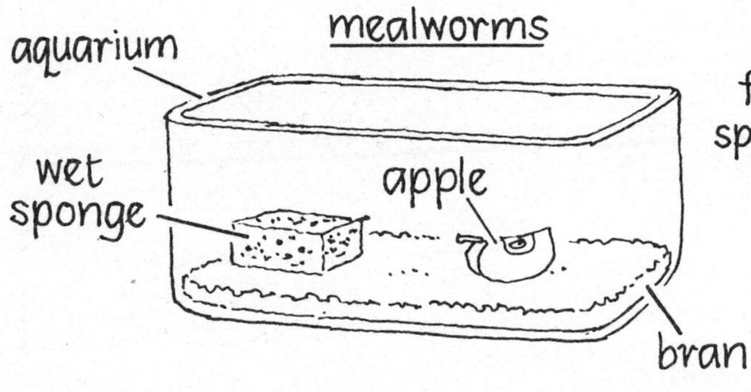

(Mealworms will happily live here for years as long as food is replaced.)

(Release tadpoles when legs start to grow as they can no longer survive in water alone.)

▲ Keep a daily diary of the changes which take place.

1 Draw and label each stage of the animal's life.

2 Write down questions you are keen to find out about.

3 Observe how the animals, move, feed and rest.

4 Do they prefer sunlight or shade?

5 Carefully measure the animals as they grow.

▲ Name ______________________________

How plants change

You will need: bean seeds; plant pot; soil.

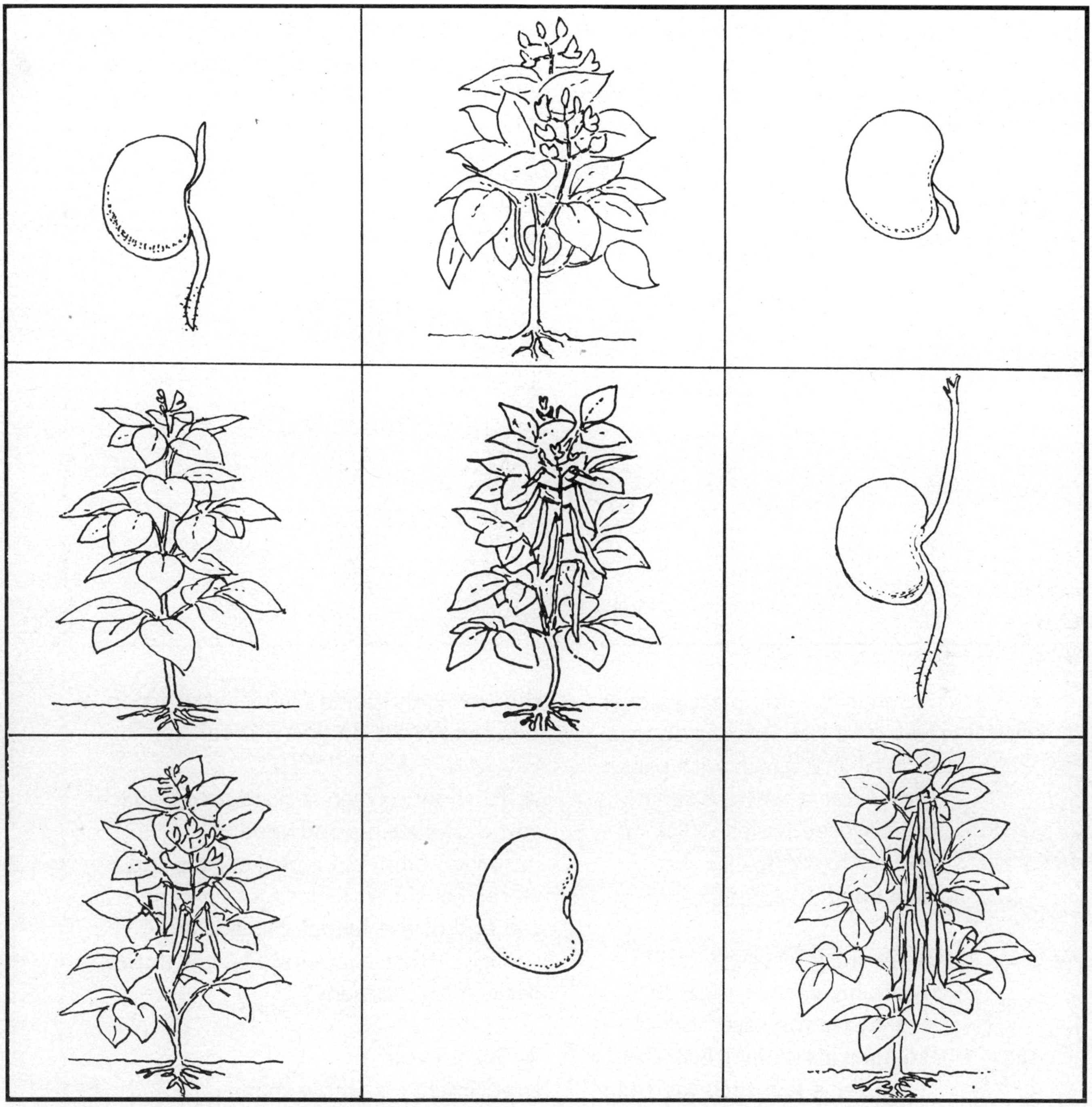

▲ How do plants change as they grow? Look at the pictures of a bean plant above. Cut out the pictures and place them in the correct order. Share you result with others. Do they agree?

▲ Plant some bean seeds in a plant pot in the classroom. Water when needed. Make a record of the plants' changes as they grow.

▲ Name ______________________

Photosynthesis

You will need: card; paper clips; water; methylated spirits; iodine; test-tube; funnel; beaker; pondweed.

Green plants are the only living things that can make their own food. They do this by using carbon dioxide from the air, water from the soil, energy from sunlight and a chemical called chlorophyll in the leaves. This process is called photosynthesis. The plant makes a type of sugar and it gives off oxygen into the air. The sugar helps the plant grow.

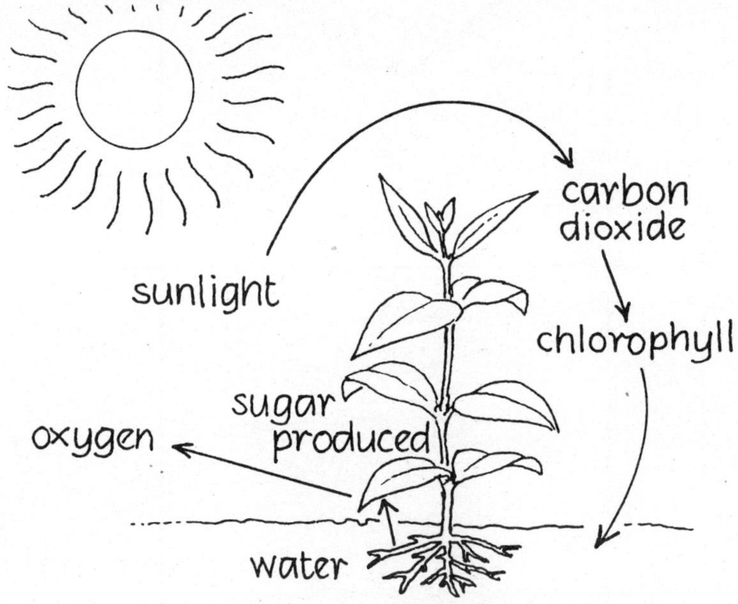

▲ Blocking sunlight – completely cover several leaves on a house-plant or tree – use card and attach with paper clips. After a week, examine the covered leaves. What do you notice? Why has this happened?

▲ Testing for sugar (starch) – cover only part of a leaf as above. Leave for several days (make sure it's sunny). Boil the leaf for a few seconds, then place the leaf in a solution of 70% methylated spirits and 30% water (an adult should do this). Now cover the leaf with iodine. (Adult supervision is needed.) What do you notice?

▲ To show oxygen is produced – place some Canadian pondweed in an upturned funnel in a beaker of pond water (as shown). Place a test-tube over the end of the funnel. Place it in sunlight. What happens? Place it in the dark. What happens?

▲ Set up your own experiments to show that plants need water and sunlight to grow. Record your results.

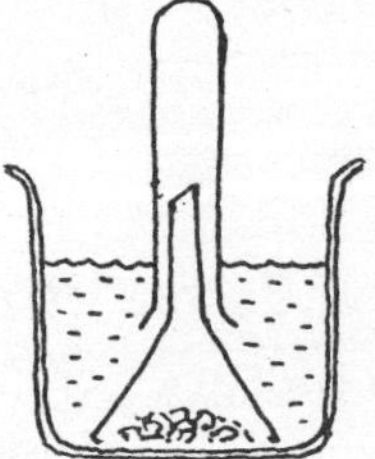

▲ Name ______________________

Will it rot?

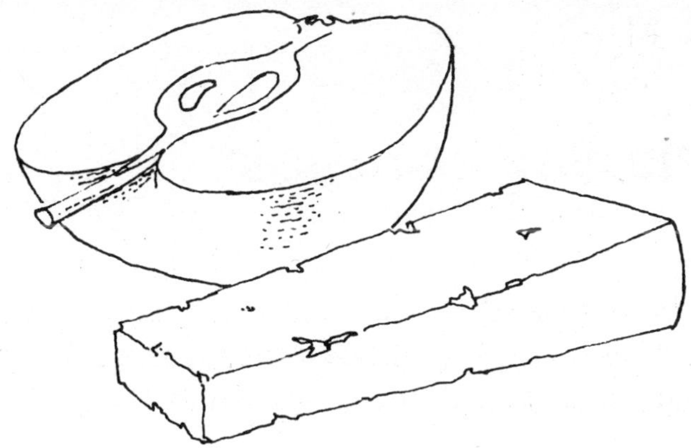

You will need: plastic food bags with ties; cheddar cheese; apples; cotton wool; water; hand lenses.

▲ Find out what happens to food kept in different conditions by doing this experiment.

1 Place a piece of cheese into three different bags.
2 Seal.
3 Place one bag in the fridge (a), one in a warm spot (b) (near a heater, sunny window ledge) and one in the room away from the sun (c).

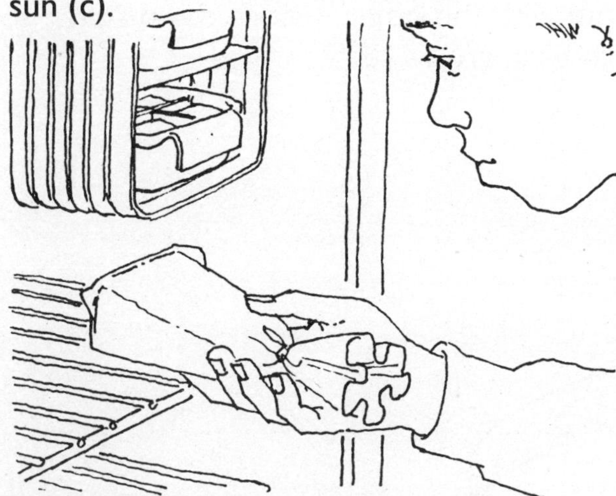

4 Do the same with pieces of apple.
5 Soak some cotton wool in water then place this in a bag with some cheese.
6 Seal.
7 In another bag, place some cheese which has been rubbed on the floor.
8 Seal.
9 Place both bags in position C.
10 Do the same with the apple.
11 Predict what might happen in each case.
▲ Record the results. Make daily observations. Note changes in colour, shape and texture.

▲ Does anything grow on the food? What is it?

Note: When observing, do not open the bags. Use a hand lens to look closely through the plastic bag.

▲ Write down the things which you think help food to rot. How can it be prevented?

▲ Name ______________________________

Making compost

You will need: plastic rubbish bin with a lid; soil; grass clippings; leaves (not evergreen); vegetable and fruit waste; garden fork.

We can change food waste, which we would normally throw away, into something useful: we can make it into compost.

▲ Try making compost yourself.

1 Make holes in the bin and lid.

2 Layer the bin as follows: grass clippings and soil, vegetable/fruit waste, rotting leaves, soil... repeating until the bin is full.

3 Put on the lid and keep the bin in a sunny spot where air can get in from the sides.

4 Mix the layers regularly with a garden fork.

▲ Observe the compost every few days. Record what happens.

▲ Try out the compost when it is ready (it will be dark and crumbly). Plant two bean seeds. Use compost on one and garden soil or sand with the other. Record the results. Which bean grows best?

repeat layers

soil

rotting leaves

vegetable/fruit waste

grass clippings and soil

▲ Name ______________________________

Genetics

Genetics is the science which studies the traits of animals and plants which are passed on to the next generation. In your own family, for example, all family members might have fair hair. As the family members grow and have their own families some of these traits may change.

▲ Find out what common traits your family has and what has been changed over the years.

▲ Try and complete as much of the table as you can. Rely on photographs and people's memories if necessary!

Family member	Colour of eyes	Colour of hair	Freckles?	Free ear-lobes?	Turned up nose?
Me					
My father					
My brother or sister					
My father's father					
My father's mother					
My father's sister or brother					
My mother					
My mother's father					
My mother's mother					
My mother's sister or brother					
My cousin					
My nephew or niece					

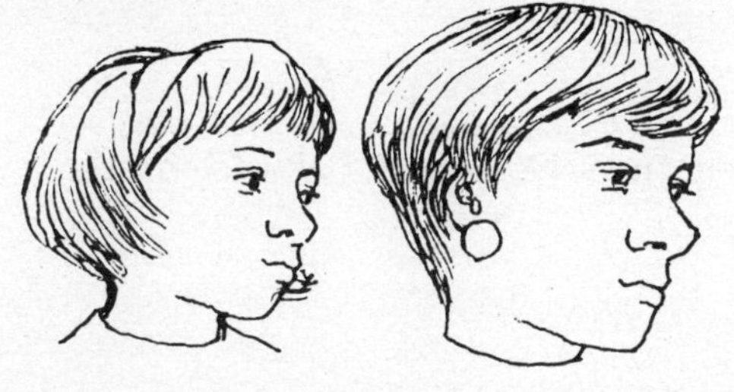

▲ Who are you most like? Does your family have a common trait or have there been changes in the way your family looks?

▲ Name ______________________

Fossils

You will need: plaster of Paris; water; Vaseline; shell; small carton such as a milk container; modelling clay; leaves.

Fossils are traces of animals or plants found in rocks. The animals and plants lived on Earth millions of years ago. Scientists use fossils to learn how living things have changed over time. They can also show how land forms have changed, for example sometimes fossils of shells are found in deserts, which tell us that the desert area was once under water.

Activity 1

Make your own fossil.

1 Mix the plaster with water until it is quite thick.
2 Pour the mixture into the carton until it is 2/3 full.
3 Coat the shell with Vaseline.
4 When the plaster begins to harden place the shell into the plaster.
5 Let it set.
6 Remove the shell.
7 Rub Vaseline over the shell dent and the top of the hard plaster.
8 Mix some more plaster of Paris and pour it into the carton.
9 When dry, lift off the top layer carefully. You have a 'fossil' cast.

Activity 2

1 Make the clay into a slab about 1 cm thick.
2 Carefully press a leaf into the clay.
3 Remove.
4 Allow the clay to harden.

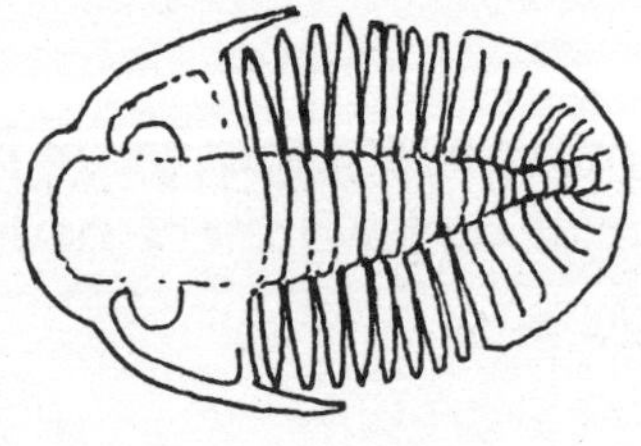

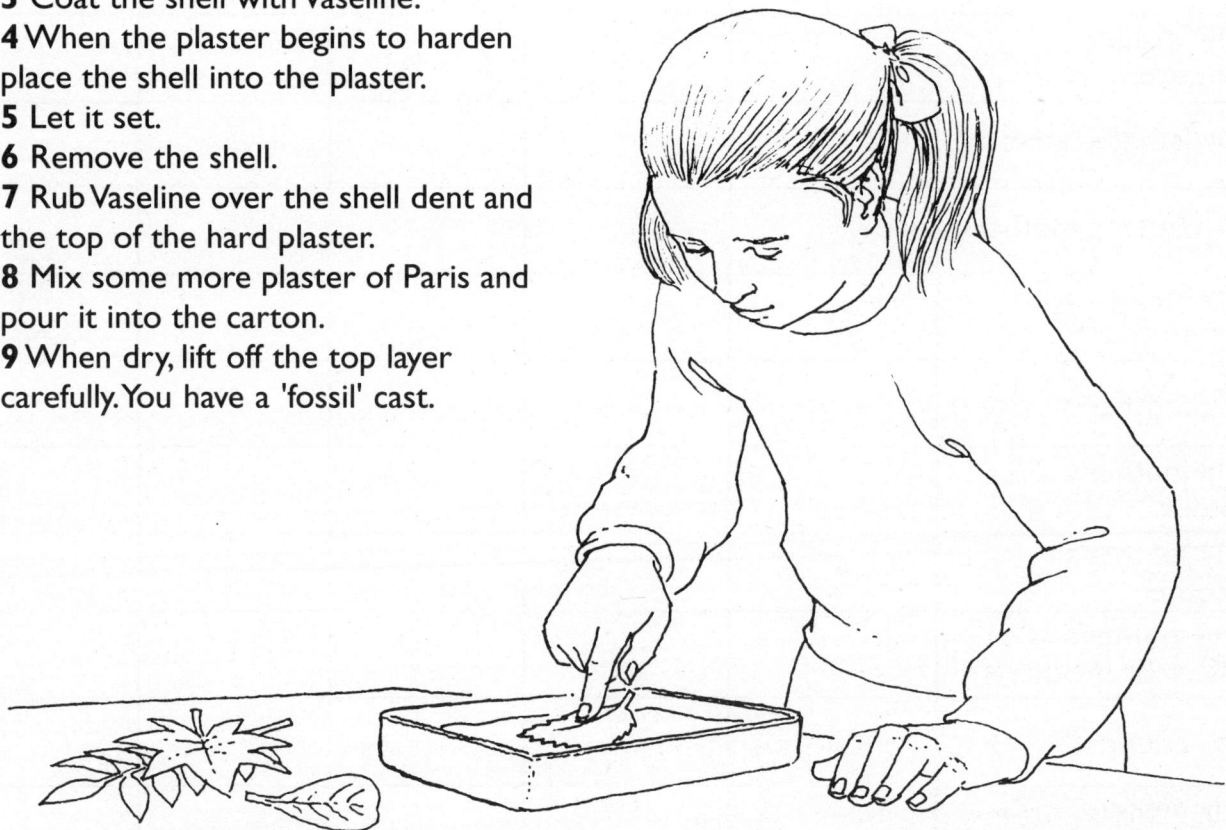

▲ Find out how real fossils are formed.

▲ Name ______________________________

Changes in the landscape – 2

Humans are able to carry out activities which can dramatically change the landscape. Sometimes these changes improve the environment for the plants and animals which live there and sometimes the changes can destroy important habitats.

▲ Look at the diagrams below. Decide whether an improvement or a destruction of the landscape has taken place. Consider also how the activities have affected the plants and animals living there.

Human activity		Your comments
1. before	after	
2. before	after	
3. before	after	

▲ Make a list of human activities which have improved or destroyed habitats for plants and animals where you live.

▲ Name ______________________

Human life cycle

You will need: a pencil.

▲ Humans grow and change as they get older. Look at the pictures below. Write down how you think the person may have changed from one age to the next.

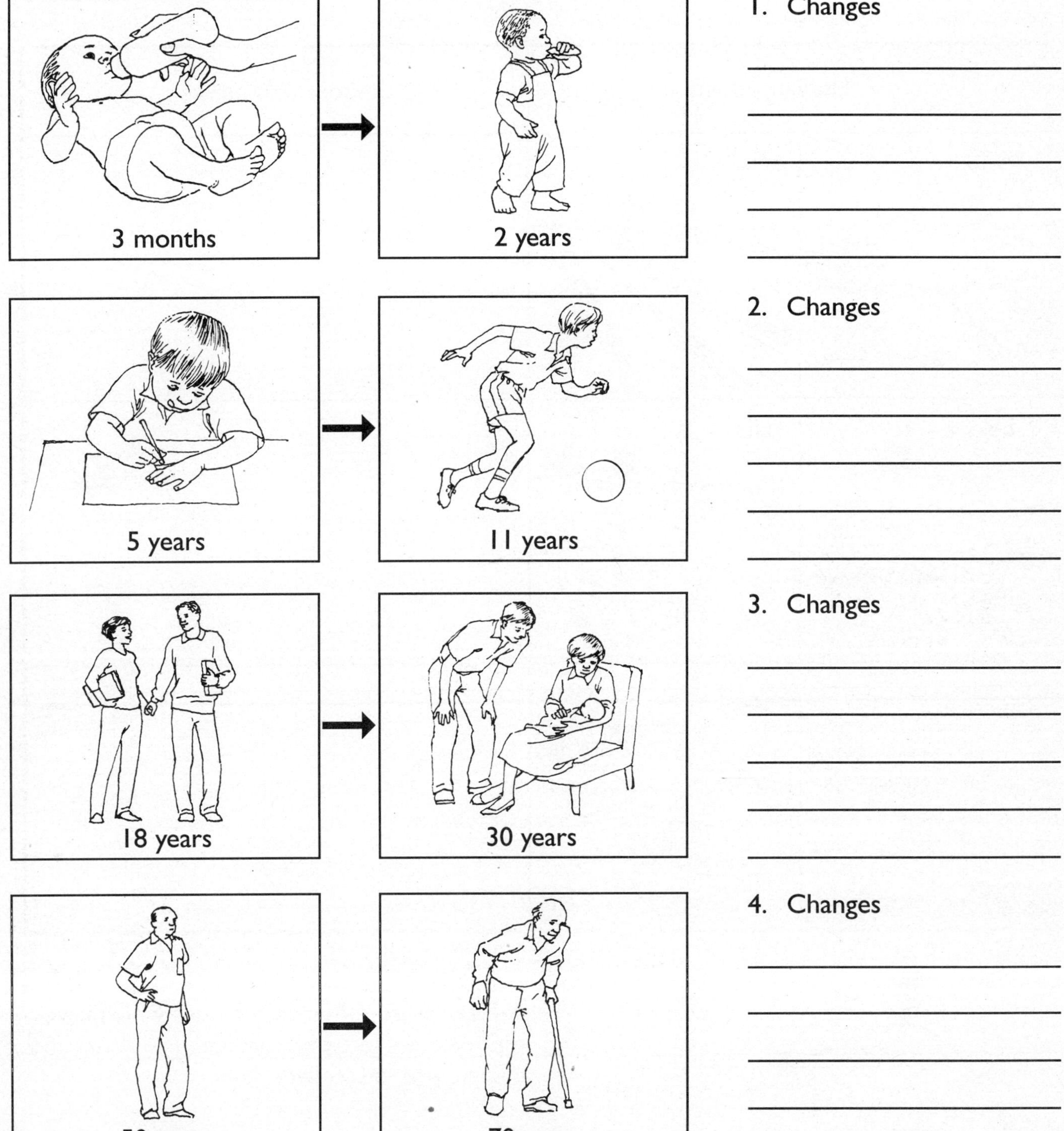

▲ Name ______________________________

Changing speed

You will need: a toy car, a thin length of rough wood, a thin length of smooth wood, large books, measuring tape, smooth floor, a pencil, some modelling clay.

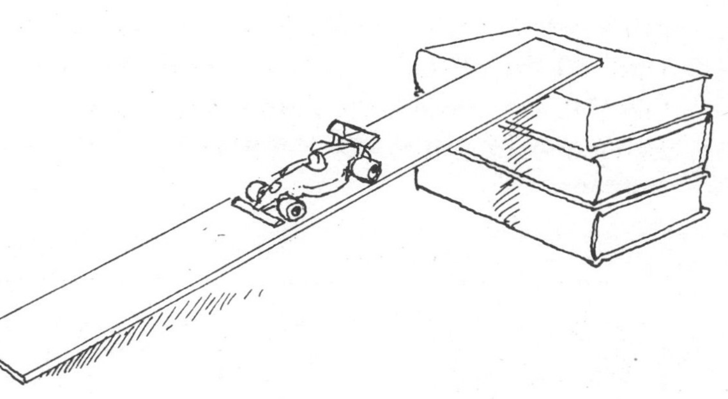

▲ Place the length of smooth wood on some books to make a ramp.
▲ Place the car on the ramp and let it go.
▲ Measure the distance it travelled from the end of the ramp to the place where the car stopped. Do this three times. Record your results.
▲ Now fix some modelling clay to the car. Do you think the car will go further or less distance now? Why? Test it out. How can you make sure it is a fair test?
▲ Try a ramp using rough wood. Record your results.

Condition	Distance travelled		
	1st try	2nd try	3rd try
smooth wood car without modelling clay			
smooth wood car with modelling clay			
rough wood car without modelling clay			
rough wood car with modelling clay			

▲ How can you explain the differences in results? How does weight affect the speed of the car?

▲ Name ______________________

The water cycle

Water is continually moving into the atmosphere by evaporation. It returns to earth in the form of snow, rain, dew and hail. On the way, water is used and changed in some way by plants and animals, including humans.

▲ Using reference books to help you, decide which word from the box describes each stage in the water cycle diagram. Some words may be used more than once.

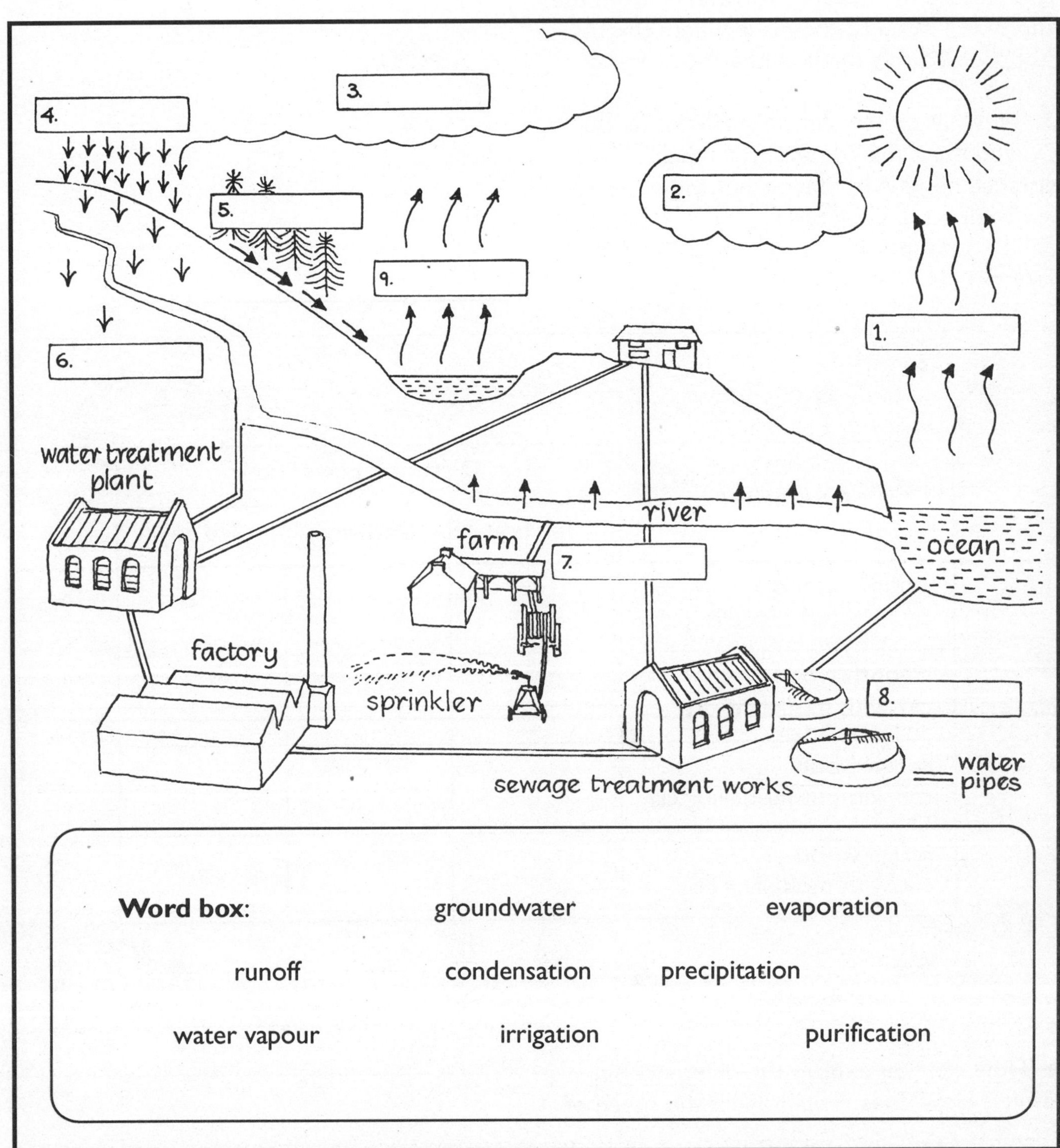

▲ Name ______________________

Changes in temperature

You will need: an alcohol thermometer.

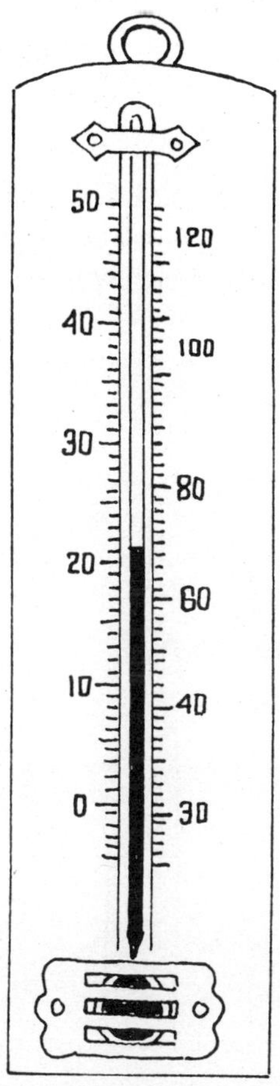

Temperature is a measure of how hot or cold something is. It is measured in degrees Celsius (^{0}C) or degrees Fahrenheit (^{0}F).
A thermometer containing mercury or alcohol is used to measure temperature.
As temperature increases, the mercury or alcohol expands in the glass tube and its level rises.
▲ Air temperature is always measured in the shade – the following experiment will help you find out why.
1 Measure the temperature in the shade and in direct sunlight at different times of the day.
2 Record your results in the chart.

▲ Which temperatures are higher? in shade? or in sun? Why do you think this is?
▲ What time of day is the hottest?
▲ Is it always hottest at this time each day?
▲ What is the average temperature for the day? for the week?

▲ If possible, record over several weeks to find the average temperature for the month.

Condition and time	Monday	Tuesday	Wednesday	Thursday	Friday
9.00am – shade					
9.00am – in sun					
10.30am – shade					
10.30am – in sun					
12.00pm – shade					
12.00pm – in sun					
3.00pm – in shade					
3.00pm – in sun					

▲ Name ______________________

Changing direction

You will need: paper, a pencil, scissors, paper clips.

▲ Use the instructions below to make a paper plane. Fly it. How well does it fly?

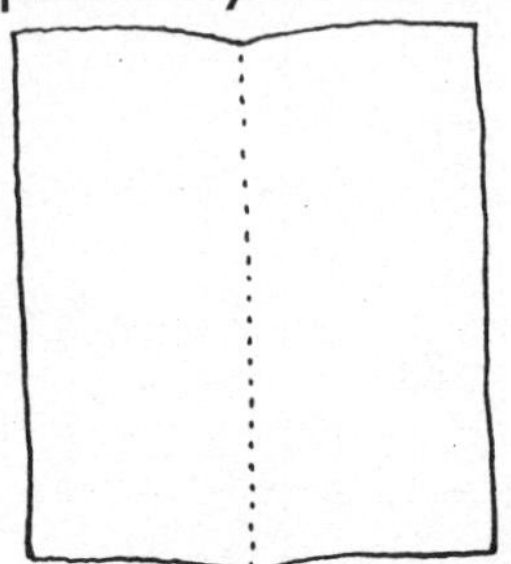

1. Fold paper in half, open out.

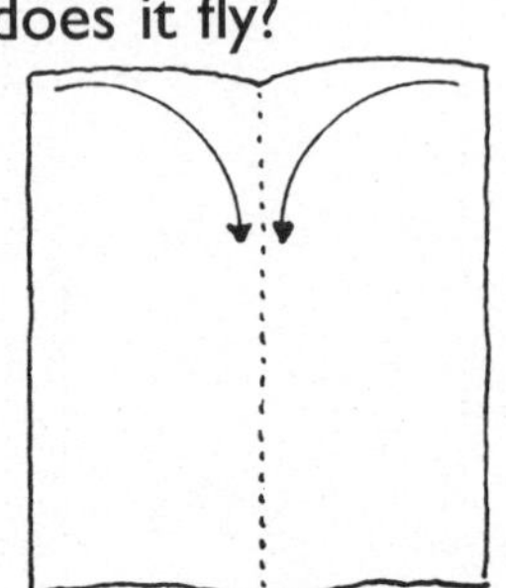

2. Fold in top corners to middle.

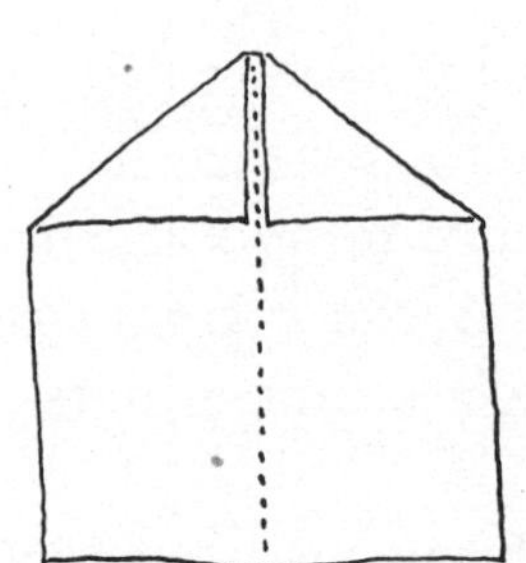

3. Fold along centre line.

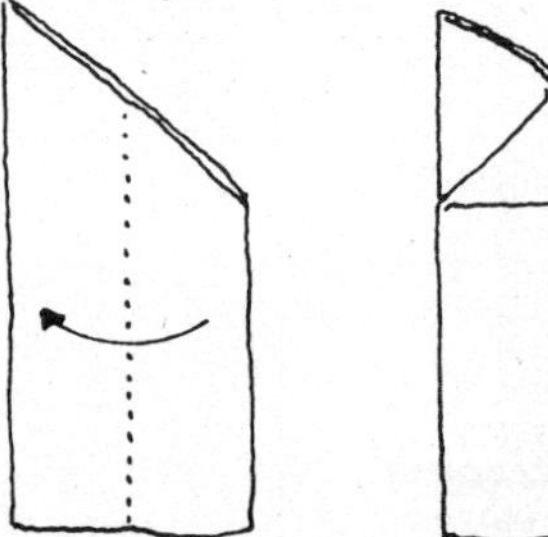

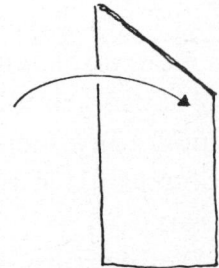

4. Fold sides down.

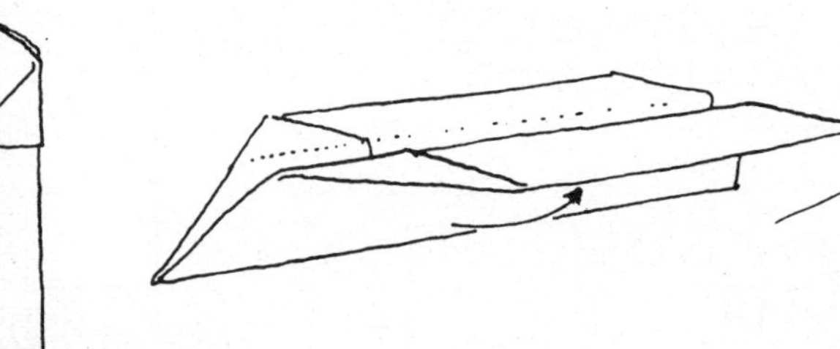

5. Open out 'wings'.

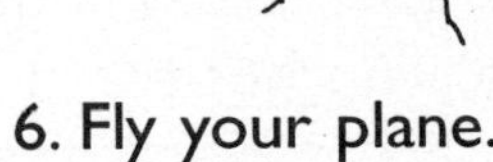

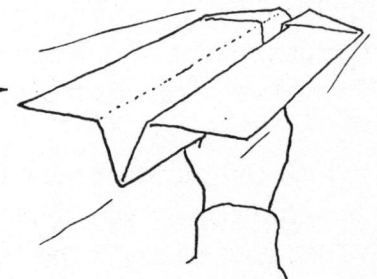

6. Fly your plane.

▲ Now make these changes to your plane. Predict first what you think might happen. Record your results.

Change	What I think will happen	What happened
Flap up on right wing		
Flap up on left wing		
Flap down on right wing		
Flap down on left wing		
Both wing flaps up		
Both wing flaps down		
Paper clip on nose		
Paper clip on tail		

▲ Try other changes. Record what happens.

▲ Name ______________________________

Shadows

You will need: a sunny day, place in playground which receives sun all day, chalk, large nail in a flat piece of wood, measuring tape, a pencil.

▲ Place the board with a nail in it on the playground in a place where it is sunny all day. Do not move it.

▲ Once every hour, visit the site. Trace the shadow with chalk. Measure the length of the shadow. Record the time and length.

▲ What changes do you notice in the shadows? Why did the shadow move round? When was the shadow shortest? Why? When was the shadow longest? Why does the length of shadow change? How effective would this shadow clock be? Would the shadow lengths change at different times of year? Why?

Time	Length of shadow

▲ Name ______________________

The seasons

The changing seasons have an effect on the plants and animals around us.
▲ Find out about the animals and plants below.

▲ Draw or write what they look like/what happens to them each season.
▲ How do the seasons affect you? Write down how you feel, what you wear, what you do for each season.

Autumn	hedgehog	beech
Winter	holly	stoat
Spring	swallow	daffodil
Summer	grass	Atlantic salmon

▲ Name ______________________________

Day and night

What changes take place with plants, animals and humans during the day and night?

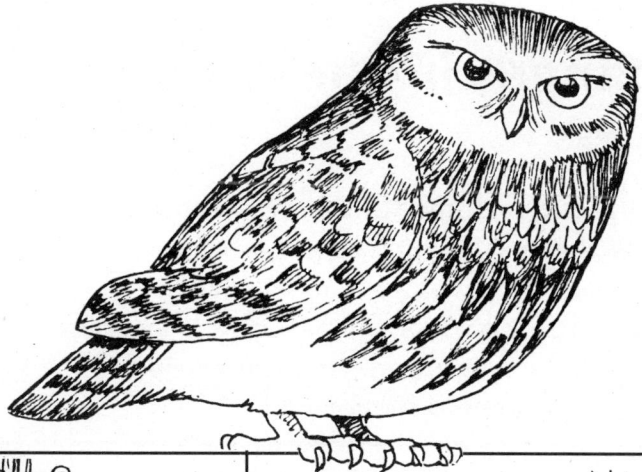

▲ Look at the pictures below. List all the changes which might occur if it was night time.

▲ Now list all the changes which might occur in these pictures if it was daytime.

▲ Record the sunrise and sunset times for one month (use newspapers or contact the meteorological station near you)

▲ Calculate the numbers of hours of daylight each day.

▲ What do you notice about the number of hours as the month progresses? Can you suggest why?

▲ Find out what causes day and night.

▲ Name ______________________

Changes in the moon

Throughout each month the moon appears to change shape. Can you suggest why?

▲ Look at each moon shape. Draw a diagram to show how this shape has been caused. The first one has been done for you.

▲ Try to watch the moon changes at night from where you live. Record the changing shapes.

Moon phase	Name of phase	Why it looks like this
	new	sun E
	crescent	
	first quarter (half)	
	gibbous	
	full	
	gibbous	
	last quarter	
	crescent	

Task 3

The right teeth for your diet

The pictures below show the skulls of two mammals. Look at the teeth.

Skull A

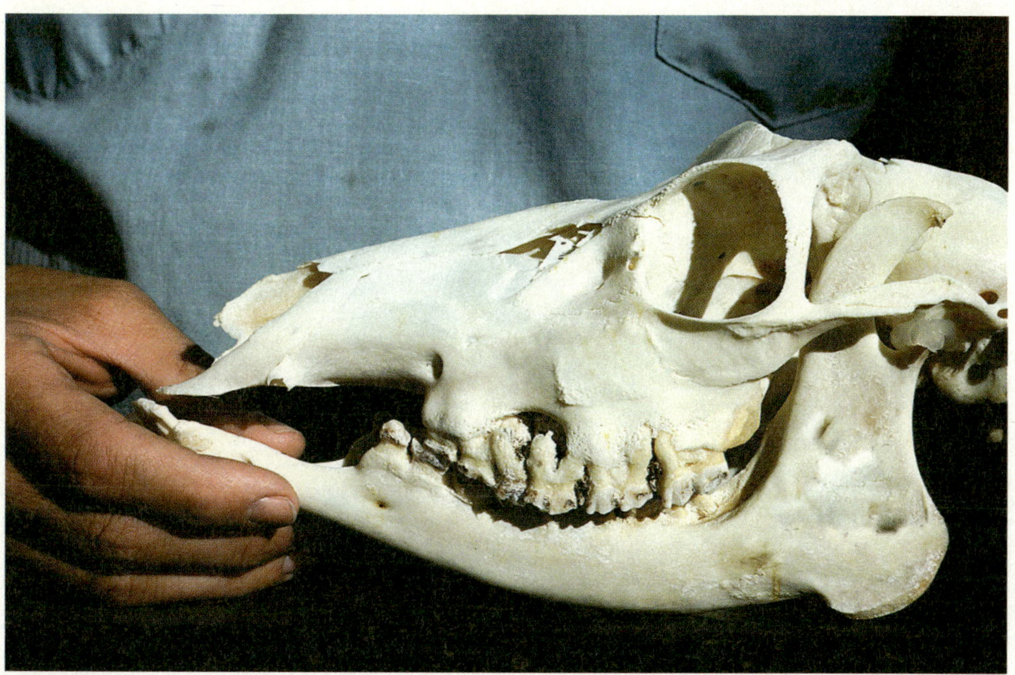

Skull B

1 What type of teeth are not present in Skull A? ______________________

2 Without these teeth, what type of food do you suggest this animal would be most likely to eat? ______________________

3 What do you call the large teeth in Skull B? ______________________

4 What is the job of these teeth? ______________________

Task 4

A healthy diet

A balanced diet has the right amounts of all the different sorts of food needed by the body.

Each of the four groups of food items shown below is a good source of something the body needs.

Michael's parents encourage him to eat foods from all these groups.

1 Write in the box next to each food group what you think it provides to keep Michael healthy. Choose from the following:

helps growth **provides energy** **protects against disease** **prevents thirst**

In science, the word 'diet' just means 'what we eat' – it doesn't mean a way to lose weight.

2 Michael's parents advise him not to eat too much of the foods shown below. Can you suggest reasons why?

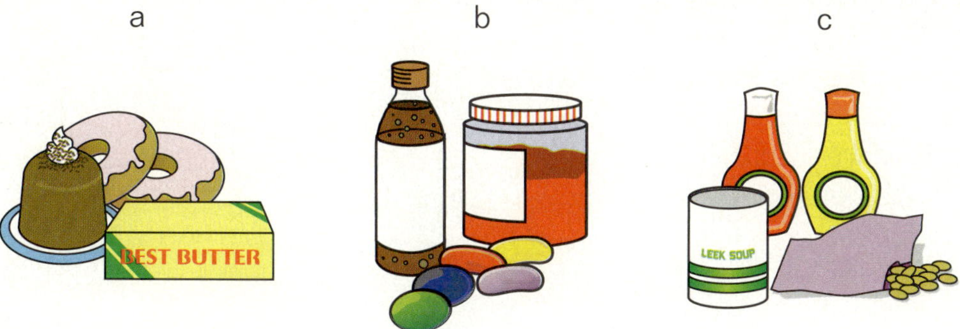

a Michael should not eat too much of the foods labelled 'a' because:

____

____

____

b Michael should not eat too much of the foods labelled 'b' because:

____

____

____

c Michael should not eat too much of the foods labelled 'c' because:

____

____

____

We get energy from fats as well as from sugars and starches.

Living together

Task 1

Making food

Plants use a special process to make their own food. Three parts of a plant help to make food from sunlight. Label the diagram below to show these three parts.

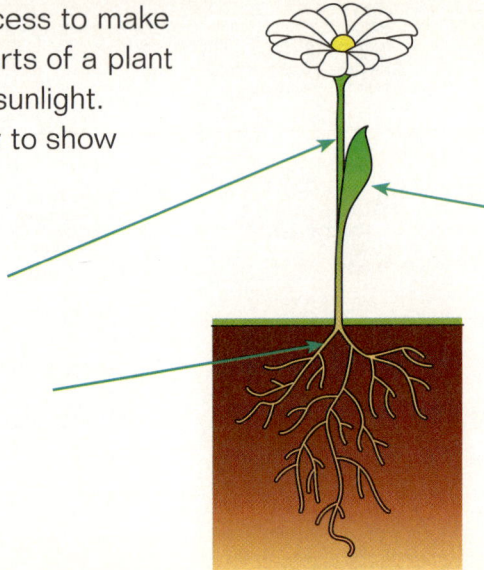

Sunlight is not food. Plants use the energy from sunlight to make food.

Task 2

Who's eating whom?

In a habitat, there can be many food chains, which connect with each other. Some animals eat more than one type of food.

The diagram below shows how some food chains connect. We call this a food web.

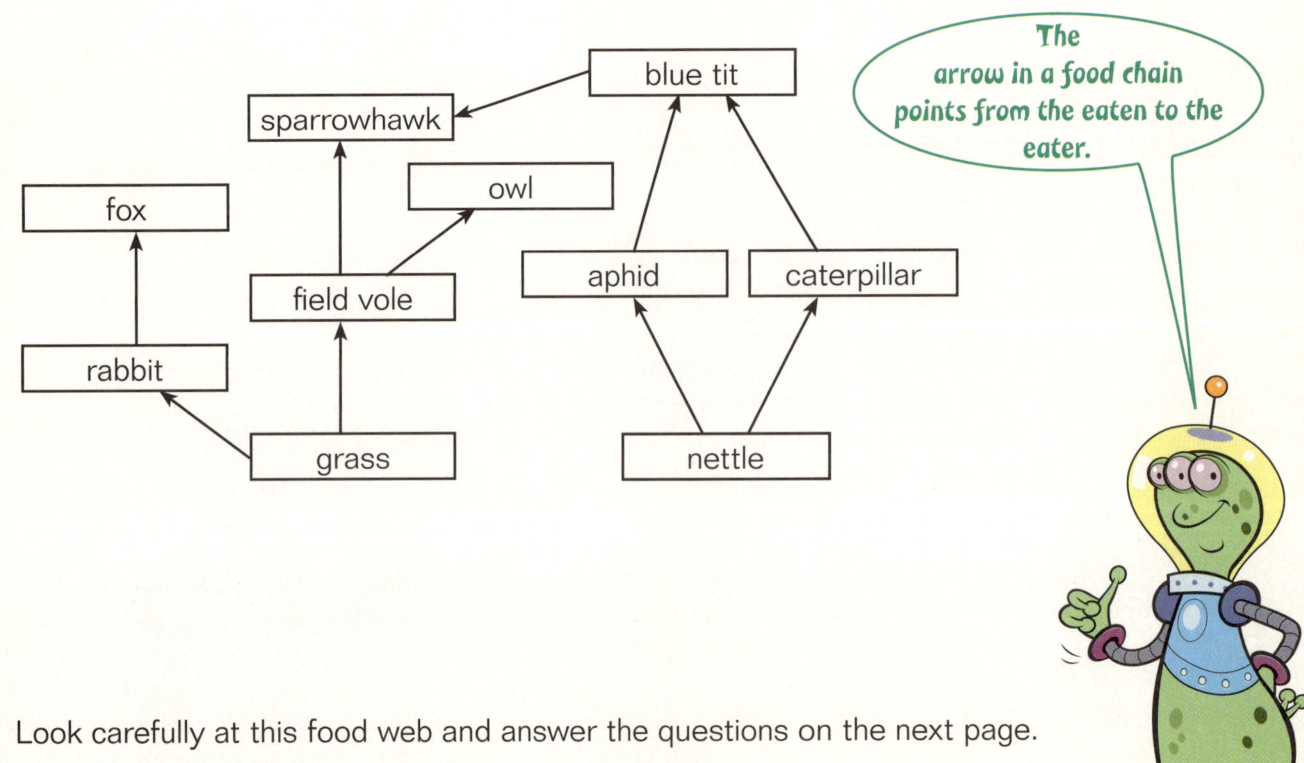

Look carefully at this food web and answer the questions on the next page.

1 Name one producer in this food web: ______________________

2 Name three consumers in this food web:

a ______________________

b ______________________

c ______________________

3 Name one herbivore in this food web: ______________________

4 Name one carnivore in this food web: ______________________

5 Name one predator in this food web: ______________________

A predator hunts and kills its prey for food.

6 Write out one food chain, beginning with a producer and containing only one consumer.

____

Most food chains begin with a green plant.

7 Construct a food chain linking three different organisms. Start with a producer.

____

8 Write out each of the three food chains in this web that lead to the sparrowhawk.

a ______________________

b ______________________

c ______________________

Task 3 Birds

The photographs show three birds that you might see on the beach or in fields close to the sea.

A

B

C

1 Use the key below to identify the three birds shown on the last page.

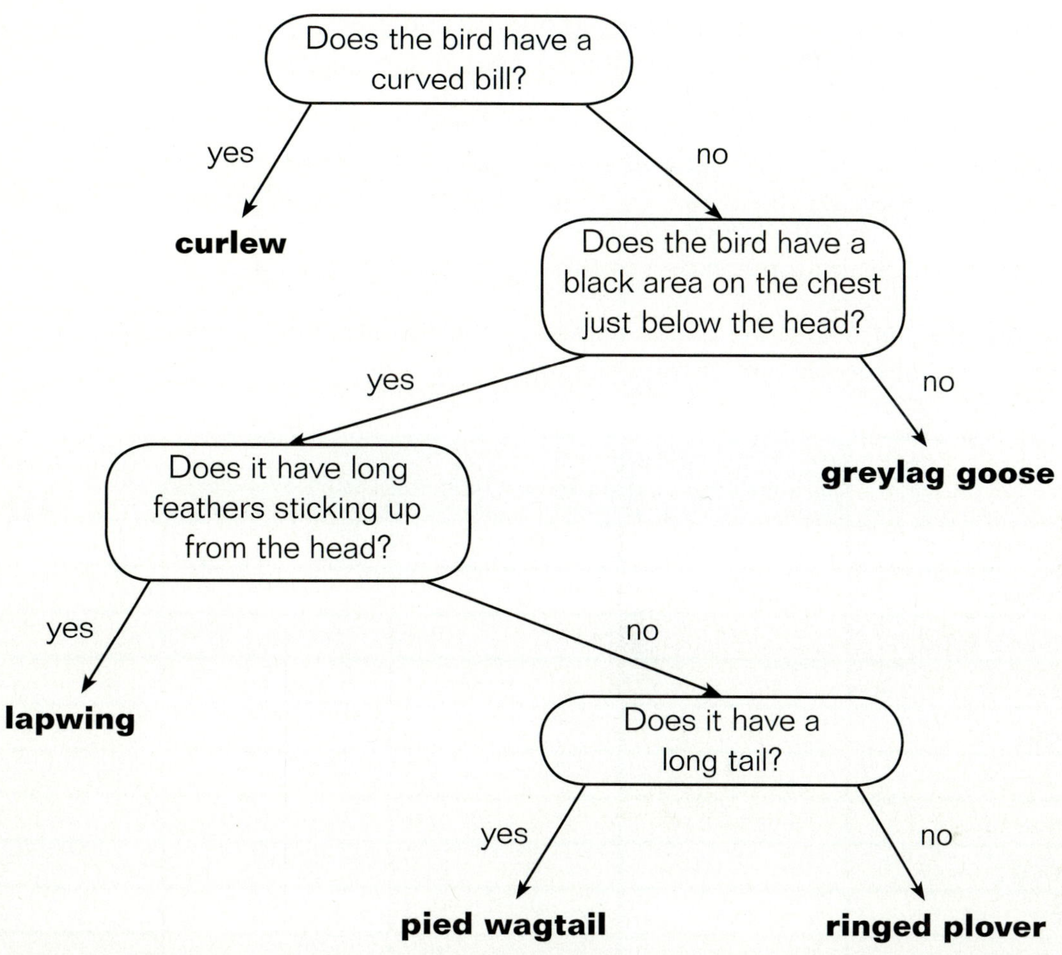
Does the bird have a curved bill?
yes
no
curlew
Does the bird have a black area on the chest just below the head?
yes
no
greylag goose
Does it have long feathers sticking up from the head?
yes
no
lapwing
Does it have a long tail?
yes
no
pied wagtail
ringed plover

a A: ____________________

b B: ____________________

c C: ____________________

2 **a** Look at the beaks of the three birds.
Which do you think would be most likely to eat worms?

____

b Give a reason for your answer.

____

____

____

Living things

Task 1 What can living things do?

Peter made a strong sugar solution by heating some water and adding sugar until no more sugar would dissolve. He then weighed a sugar cube and suspended it in the solution. After two weeks, he found that the sugar cube had grown in size and mass.

He thought about what he had learned about animals and plants: *'Animals and plants grow… they are living things. The sugar cube also grew, so are sugar crystals also living things?'*

1 Working with the rest of your group, put a tick in the table below wherever **all** the things named at the top can do the thing described on the left.

2 Decide whether or not the things named at the top of each column are living, and write 'yes' or 'no' at the bottom of the column.

	all plants	all animals	all crystals	all clockwork toys
grow in size				
reproduce				
make own food				
move				
lay eggs				
fly				
swim				
eat food				
respire				
get rid of waste				
Are they living?				

A cloud moves. Is it a living thing?

Task 2 Making a key

Here is a plan for writing a key to help identify birds, fish, mammals and insects.

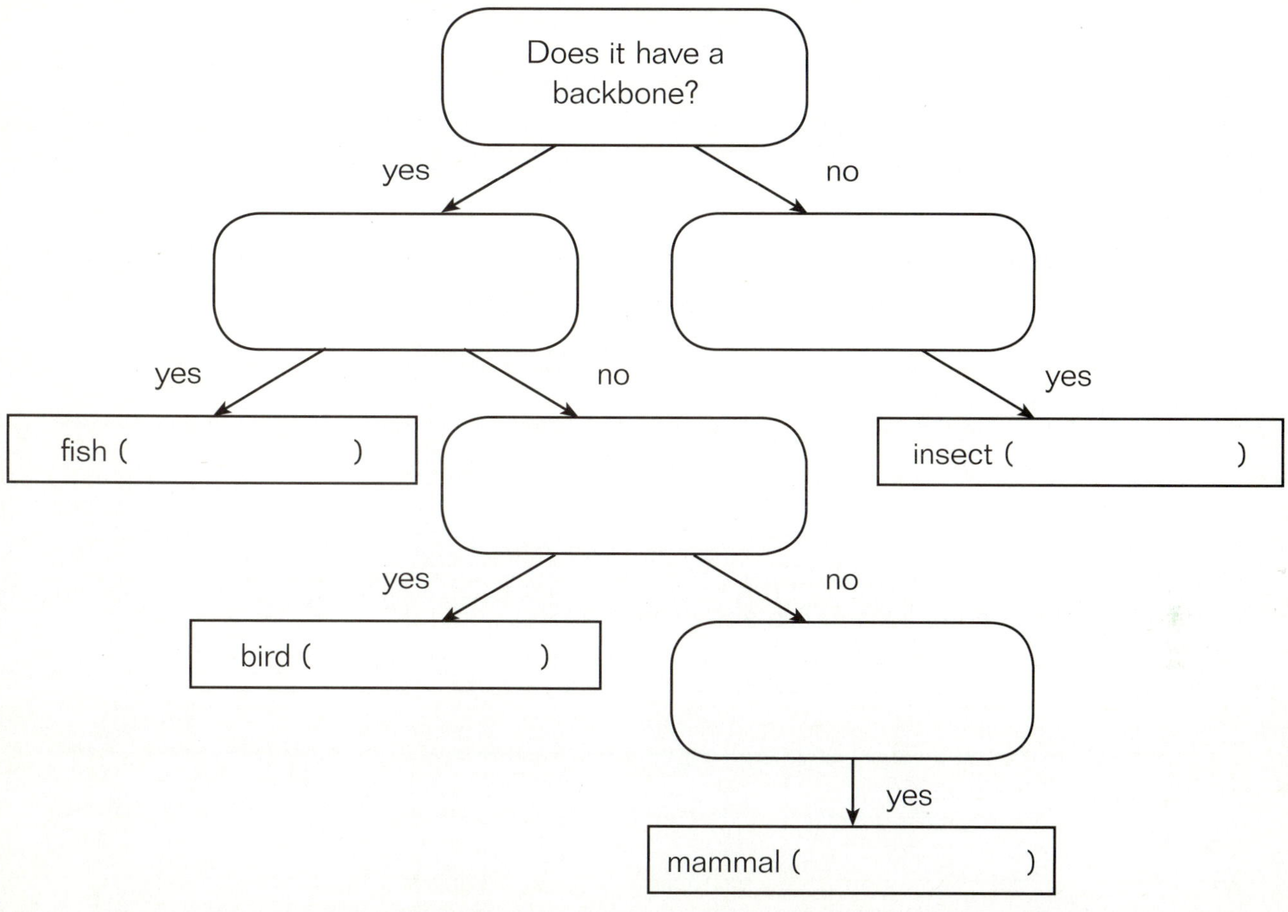

1 Here are some questions that you could use to complete the key. Discuss them with your partner and decide what you should write in each box.

- 'Does it have feathers, a beak and two legs?'
- 'Does it feed its young with milk and have fur or hair?'
- 'Does it have gills, scales and fins?'
- 'Does it have three body parts, an outside skeleton and six jointed legs?'

Be careful: sometimes the common names of animals are misleading. A jellyfish is not a fish!

2 Write your name in the brackets after the name of the group that you belong to.

Task 3 Plants and animals

Here are some questions about plants and animals.
Write your answers in the spaces provided.

1 Animals need water to live and grow.
Name two other things they need to live and grow.

a ______________________________

b ______________________________

2 All living things reproduce.
What would happen if living things did not reproduce?

____

____

____

____

3 Why do plants need light to live and grow?

____

____

____

____

4 Do animals need light for the same reason as plants?
Explain your answer.

____

____

____

____

Task 4

Overcrowding

Four groups of children want to find out how overcrowding can affect the way plants grow. They plant similar bean seedlings in pots of the same size. They place the pots in the same part of the garden. Each pot is given the same amount of water.

These are the experiments of the groups A, B, C, and D:

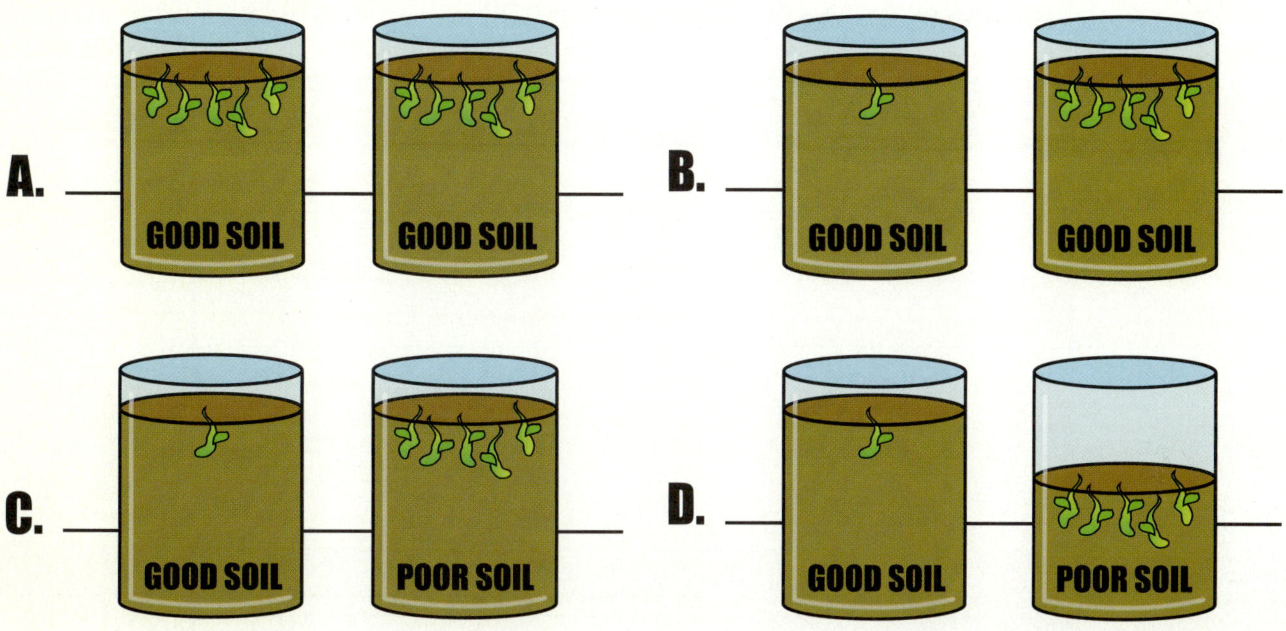

1 In the table below, tick the factors that are being compared in each group's experiment.

Group	Number of plants	Kind of soil	Amount of soil
A			
B			
C			
D			

2 Which group has planned a fair test?

____

3 What would you predict that the results of this group's experiment would show?

____

____

____

Task 5

Gain in height

Some children asked their teacher: 'Do we grow more quickly at some times than at others?'

The teacher showed them these two bar charts.
They show the average gain in height of boys and girls in each year from ages 6 to 18.

Use the bar charts to answer the questions on the next page.

Height increase by age (girls)

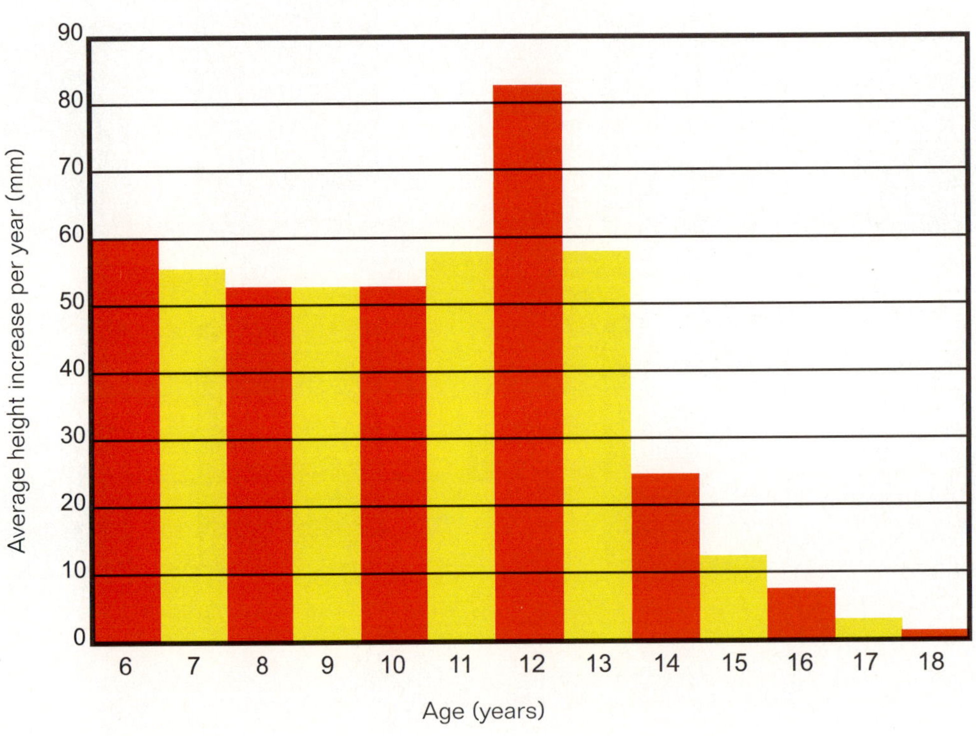

Height increase by age (boys)

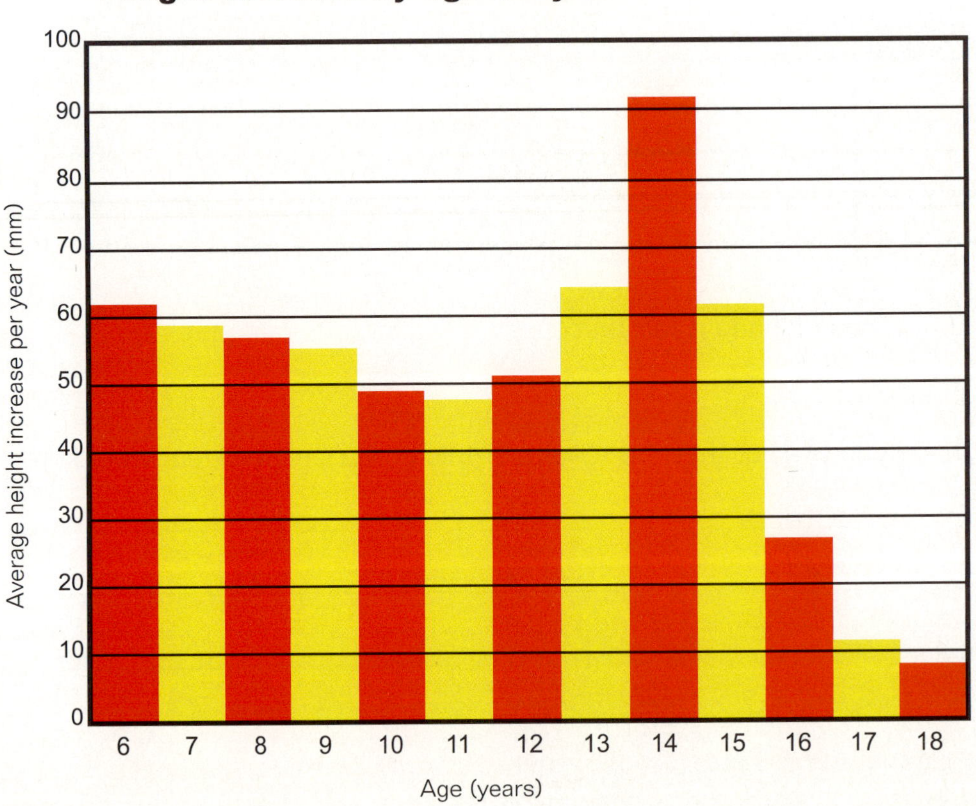

Writing tests

- **How to help your child do well in the Writing tests:**
- **Ensure they read lots of different things!!**
- **Make good use of planning time**
- **Practise reading their piece of writing, looking for:**
- a mix of long and short sentences using a range of connectives
- a brisk pace of story
- use of appropriate layout to task
- a clear beginning, middle and end
- use of interesting language (like 'muttered' instead of 'said') WOW words!
- Accurate and varied punctuation
- all verbs agreeing
- making sure the piece **matches the title**
- **VCOP/PEE!**

Maths tests

- Always need to **show how got to the answer**, even when used a calculator (might get a mark even for a wrong answer)
- The questions get harder, so double check the early ones before attempting the really tricky ones at the back
- Many questions are written as 'real' problems. Practice drawing the answer, (jottings) especially with division sums (eg, sharing out can be done into the right number of circles)
- **Know all times tables and division facts**
- **Ask for questions to be read – there is no shame in this at all.**
- **Look out for 'trick' questions e.g. which numbers are NOT factors of 50**

Science tests

- Read graphs and charts accurately
- In questions asking for a general rule, use this sentence structure: 'The .... the... the... the ...,' eg.'The thicker the string the lower the pitch.' This is more likely to get two marks than a paragraph of waffle
- Practise reading the questions carefully
- The paper is a test of knowledge, so read those revision guides!
- Children will be assessed on how they manage and think about Scientific Enquiry. This will involve them thinking about an investigation or experiment and answering questions about the described activity.

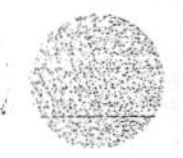

How else you can help?

SATs can be a worrying time for your child and s/he may get nervous as the tests loom ahead. Good coping strategies include:

- **Reassuring that you love them, whatever!**
- **Encouraging them to spend 20 minutes a day on revision or practice**
- **Reminding them that in many parts of the SAT papers, children do not have to write in sentences: often, phrases or even single words will be enough**
- **Teaching them how to relax by breathing deeply and closing their eyes to picture a calm scene like a green field by a river**
- **Making sure they have breakfast every day, especially during the week of the tests - children who miss breakfast perform worse in late morning**
- **Checking they can tell the time accurately, so they know how long there is to go in the test. We give lots of time checks.**
- **Making sure they get plenty of sleep**
- **Making sure they live their life!**
- **Reassuring that you love them, whatever!**

Your questions

Wednesday 12th March 2008

Preparing for KS2 SATS

Getting Ready

- The biggest single influence on your child's SAT marks will be her reading ability. Good readers can read questions quickly, and understand what they need to do. **Encourage your child to read every day, looking at both stories and non-fiction.**
- Children who find reading difficult can have questions read to them in Maths and Science **but they must ask question by question** – they only have to put up their hand.

General tips for children's well -being

- SATs are important for the child and the school but not worth sacrificing health and emotional well – being for
- Together we need to encourage the children to do their best, pulling out all the stops until May.

Timetable

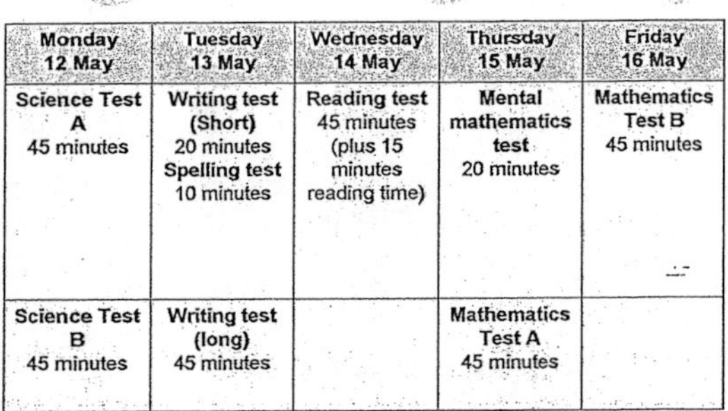

Monday 12 May	Tuesday 13 May	Wednesday 14 May	Thursday 15 May	Friday 16 May
Science Test A 45 minutes	**Writing test (Short)** 20 minutes **Spelling test** 10 minutes	**Reading test** 45 minutes (plus 15 minutes reading time)	**Mental mathematics test** 20 minutes	**Mathematics Test B** 45 minutes
Science Test B 45 minutes	**Writing test (long)** 45 minutes		**Mathematics Test A** 45 minutes	

Reading Test

- **15 minutes to read the texts, so practise concentrating on careful reading for that time** – no distractions!
- Allowed to make notes on the reading booklet, which will not be marked. So, encourage them to underline:
- key events in the story
- words which show what a character is like
- key facts
- anything which suggests time of day (like 'low sun' would be morning or evening)
- phrases they like - handy if there is a question asking for an opinion on the story
- **Practice doing this every time they read at home.**
- These annotations could help them find their way around the text quickly when answering questions.
- Read each question twice. It doesn't take long, and will aid in understanding what they need to do each time. Questions in this part of the test often ask 'Which part of the story tells us that...' - so they will need to quote, or summarise that part of the story to answer properly. Remind them to try all questions, which do not necessarily get harder through the test.

Writing tests

- Children will complete two tests:
- The Short Writing Test will last 20 minutes and children will have to complete a piece of writing in that time. E.g. an opening paragraph of a story
- The Long Writing Test will last about 45 minutes. Children will need to write a longer piece including spending up to 15 minutes planning. E.g. a persuasive leaflet

1 Between which ages does the first graph show that girls grow at a constant rate?

2 At what age does the first graph show that girls grow fastest?

3 At what age does the second graph show that boys grow fastest?

4 Boys and girls usually start to grow faster when they reach adolescence.
Use the graphs to decide whether boys or girls usually reach adolescence earlier.

Human body

Task 1 What does this organ do?

On the left below are some organs in the human body, and on the right are some functions. Next to each organ, write the letter to show what it does. The first has been done for you.

eye	E	A	helps to digest food
brain	_	B	detects smells to give sense of smell
lung	_	C	interprets messages
ear	_	D	pumps blood around the body
skin	_	E	detects light to give sense of sight
stomach	_	F	detects sound to give sense of hearing
nose	_	G	protects against infection
heart	_	H	enables exchange of oxygen and carbon dioxide

Task 2 Your heart

This diagram shows the circulation of blood through the human body.

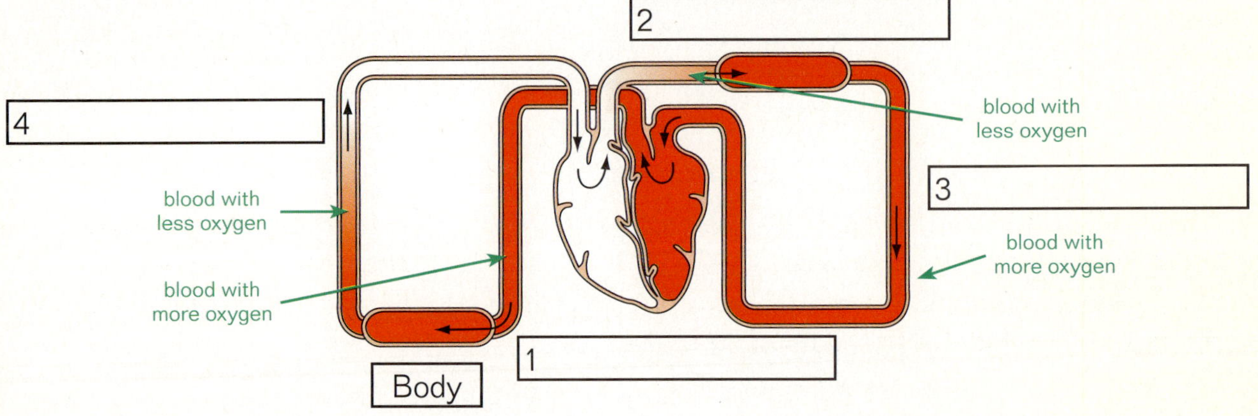

1 In box 1, write the name of the organ in the middle of the diagram.

2 Describe what this organ does. ______________________

3 In box 2, write the name of the organ where blood takes in oxygen.

4 In each of boxes 3 and 4, write either 'arteries' or 'veins'.

5 What does your pulse rate measure? ______________________

6 Name two places where you can measure your pulse. __________ __________

7 State two things you can do to keep your heart healthy.

______________________ ______________________

8 Name the part of the skeleton that protects the heart and lungs. ______________

Task 3 Muscle action

Jack and Jamie were studying how muscles help in movement.
They could feel two muscles in their upper arm.

1 They observed how the muscles in their upper arm worked.
As Jamie lifted a very heavy book, Jack observed a bulge in one of Jamie's muscles.

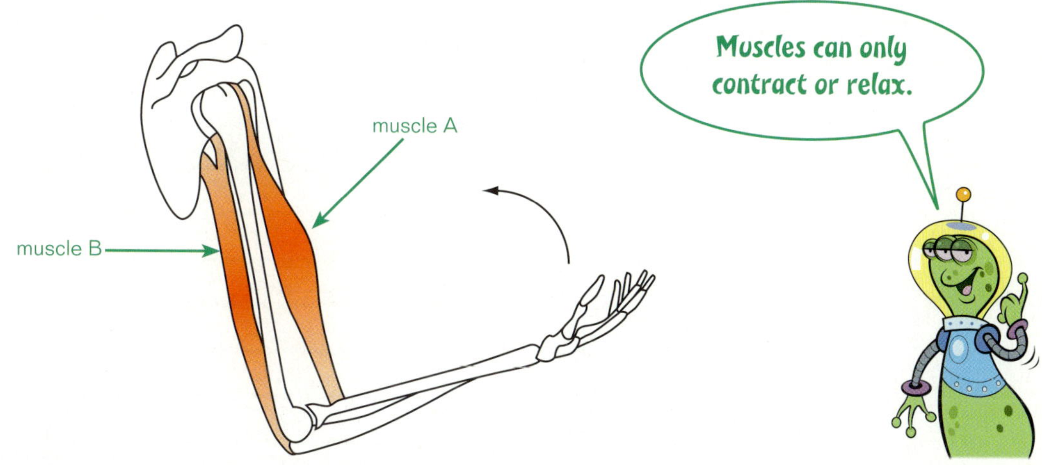
muscle A
muscle B
Muscles can only contract or relax.

a Did Jack observe the bulge in muscle A or muscle B? ______________

b What happens to the other muscle as this muscle contracts? ______________

c Jamie left the book on a table and lowered his arm as he walked away.
Describe how the muscles worked as Jamie lowered his arm.

____

d Describe what a joint is. ____

____

2 Muscles work in pairs. Jamie and Jack made a model to show the action of muscles on the bones they are attached to. They used thick card to represent the bones of the forearm and upper arm and rubber bands to represent muscle A and muscle B. Compare the model with the drawing above.

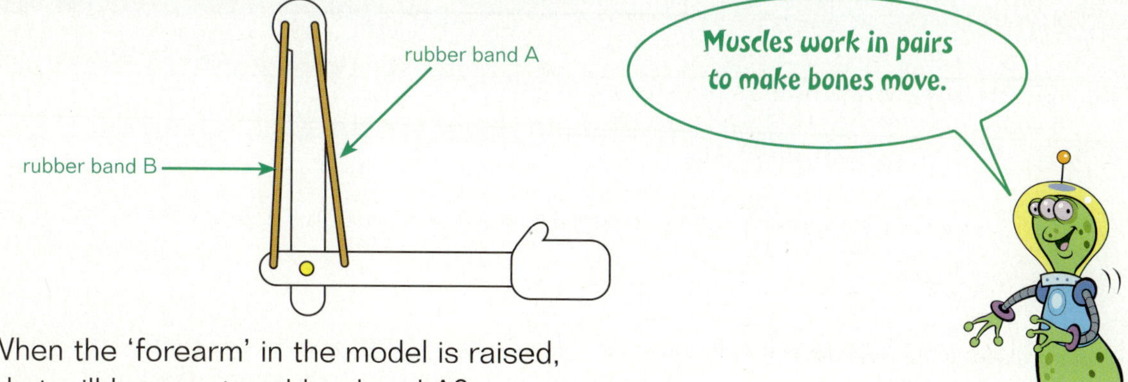
rubber band A
rubber band B
Muscles work in pairs to make bones move.

a When the 'forearm' in the model is raised, what will happen to rubber band A?

____

b How is this different from the way real muscles work?

____

Task 4

Exercise and heart rate

During a PE lesson, Samantha's teacher wanted to show the class the effect of exercise on heart rate. First she measured Samantha's heart rate when she was resting.

Samantha then skipped energetically for 2 minutes. Her teacher measured her heart rate as soon as she stopped skipping, and continued to take measurements at one-minute intervals until her heart rate returned to the resting rate.

The class recorded the measurements, as shown in the table below.

Time	Heart rate (beats per minute)
resting before exercise	70
immediately after exercise	145
1 minute after exercise	135
2 minutes after exercise	125
3 minutes after exercise	115
4 minutes after exercise	95
5 minutes after exercise	85
6 minutes after exercise	75
7 minutes after exercise	70

1 What was Samantha's heart rate before she started skipping? ______________

2 What happened to Samantha's heart rate when she was skipping? Explain your answer.

____

____

____

____

____

____

3 How long did it take for her heart rate to return to normal? ______________

4 The teacher also recorded Yasmin's heart rate before and after exercise. Yasmin's resting heart rate was 70 beats per minute. Yasmin plotted her results in a graph.

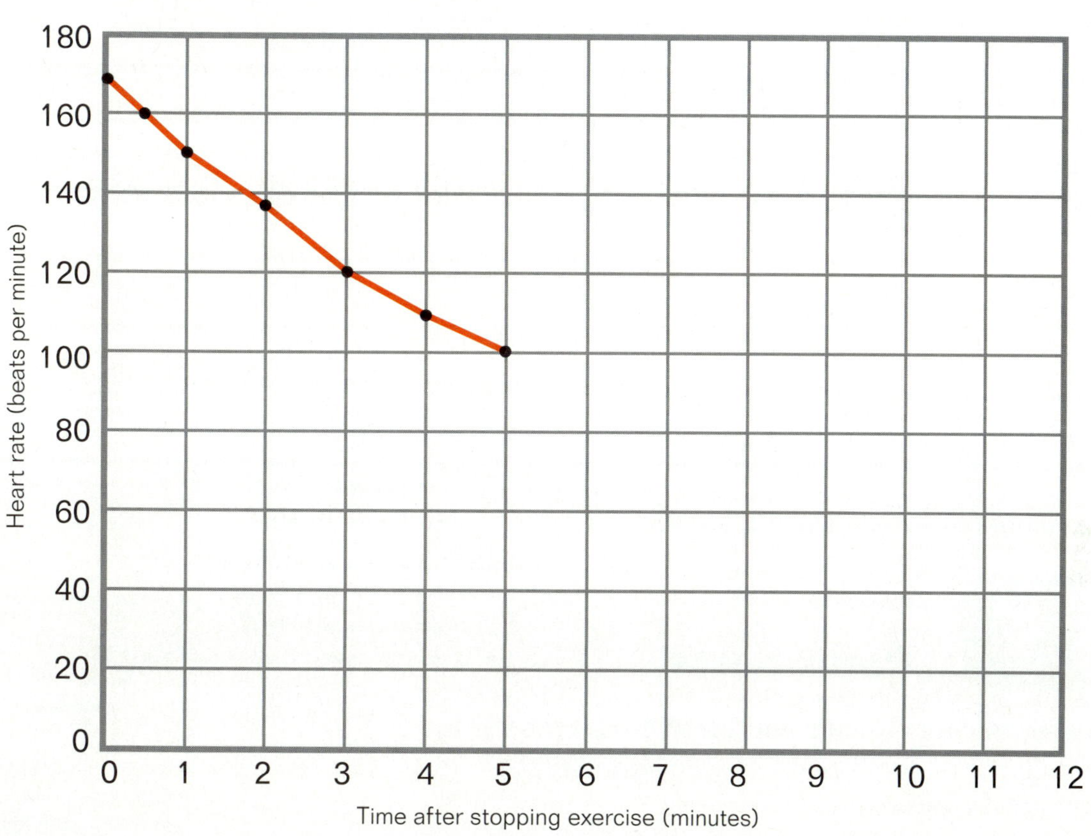

Continue the line on the graph to show Yasmin's heart rate returning to its resting rate.

Our muscles work harder during exercise than when we are sitting still.

5 Estimate when Yasmin's heart rate will return to its resting rate. ______________

Growing plants

Task 1 What I think it does

What do you think the following parts of a plant do? Discuss your answers with your group, before you share them with your teacher and the other groups.

Part of plant	What it does
root	
stem or trunk	
leaf	
fruit	
seed	

Task 2 Plant parts

Here are some clues to help you complete a crossword on the functions of some parts of a flowering plant. Try to do this crossword on your own.

Roots absorb water and minerals, but not food. Plants make their own food.

Across

3 Where the reproductive organs of a plant are.

4 Lets the plant grow up towards the light.

Down

1 Absorb water and minerals from the soil.

2 Makes food for the plant.

3 Develops after fertilisation.

4 Part of the plant that will grow into a new plant.

			1			
					2	
	3					
4						

Task 3

Reproduction

Mary was revising the parts of a flower. She labelled the diagram as shown below.

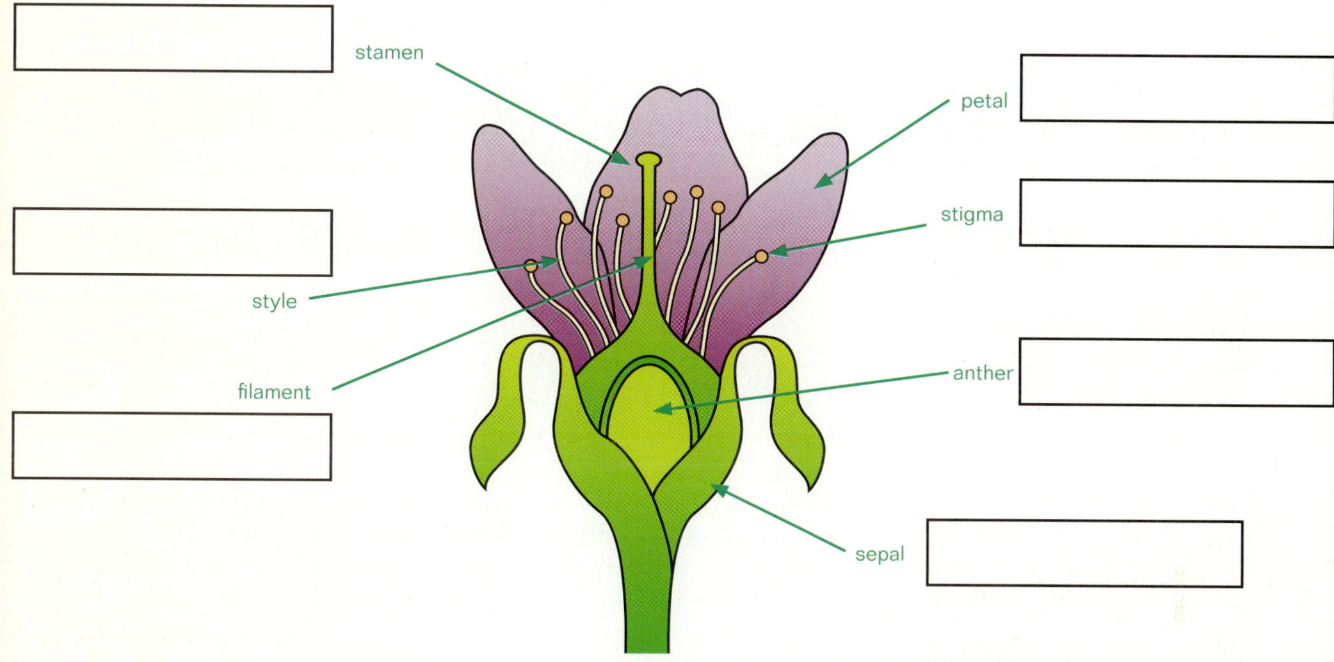

The stamen contains pollen. Pollen are not seeds.

Can you correct Mary's answers?
Put a tick in the box if you think Mary has the right answer.
Write the correct name in the box if you think Mary has the wrong answer.

What are the female parts of a flower called? ____________________

Task 4 Germination

Ali placed a few green-bean seeds in a jar containing some damp cotton wool.
He placed the jar on a sunny window sill.
He made sure the cotton wool was kept damp and observed the jar every day for two weeks.

Most seeds do not need light to germinate, but they do need warmth.

After 14 days, Ali found his seeds had germinated and developed into seedlings.

1 What are the three conditions for germination that Ali has provided?

________________ ________________ ________________

2 Ali said the seedlings were now ready to be planted out in the garden.
He wanted to observe the stages in the life cycle of his bean plant.
In the table below, write the order of these stages, starting with the seedling stage.

Order	Stage in life cycle
1	seedling grows bigger
	flower forms
	plant reaches adult stage
	fertilisation takes place in the ovary
	seeds are dispersed
	flower is pollinated
	seeds are formed
	fruit ripens
	seed germinates

Seeds are formed in the flower.

Task 5

Dandelion seeds

The drawing shows some dandelion seeds. Each seed is small and light, and has fine hairs at one end. Each hair is called a pappus.

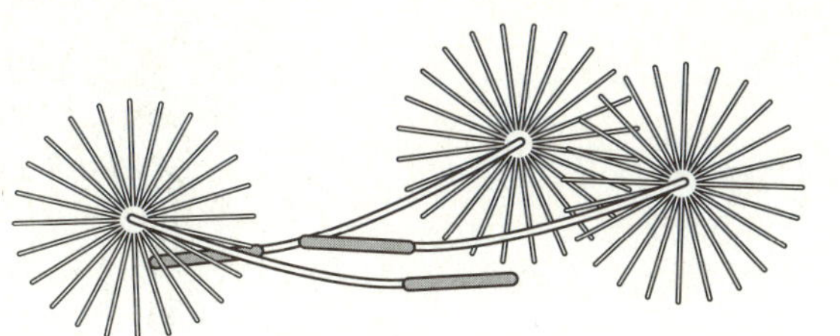

Seeds are living things.

1 How do you think the dandelion disperses its seeds?

____

2 Why do plants need to disperse their seeds?

____

3 David and Michael carried out the following investigation. They collected 10 dandelion seeds. They set up a fan spinning at a constant speed. They stood at a fixed distance from the fan and dropped a seed from a fixed height. They measured the distance the seed travelled. They repeated this for 10 seeds, and recorded the distances travelled.

Next they removed all the hairs from the 10 seeds, and repeated what they had done.

They used a table like the one below to record their results.

	Distance travelled										
seed	1	2	3	4	5	6	7	8	9	10	average
with pappus											
without pappus											

a What question were they trying to answer?

____

b Why did they do the experiment with 10 seeds rather than just one?

____

____

Taking measurements several times is not the same as making a fair test.

c Why did they work out the average distance?

____

____

d What do you think they concluded?

____

Sc3 Materials and their properties

Using materials

Task 1

Which material?

Circle the name of the material that would be best for each item indicated below.

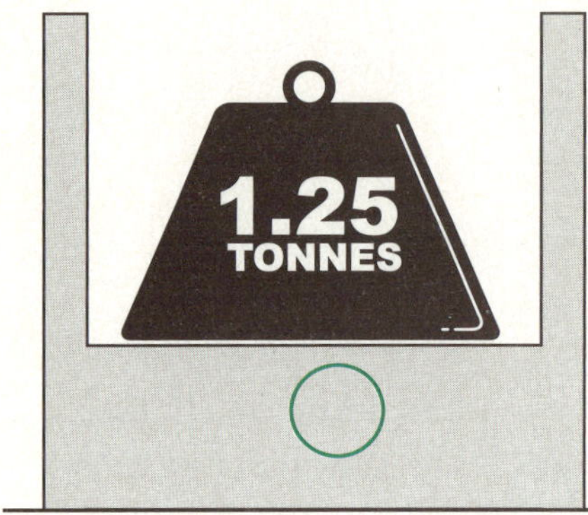

sponge

concrete

polystyrene

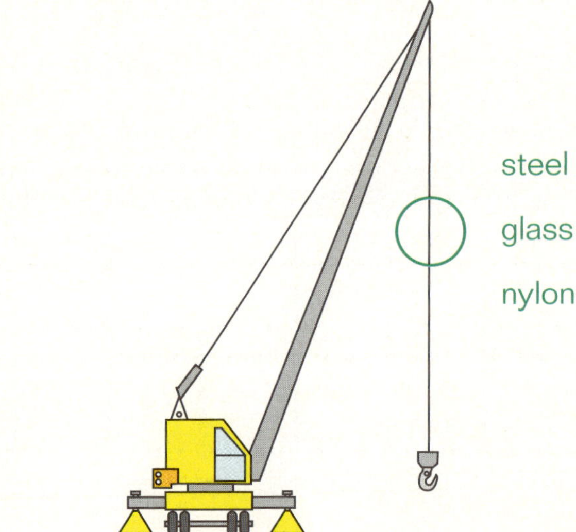

steel

glass

nylon

wood

glass

rubber

For each of your answers, explain why it is the best material and give another example of something that could be made from the same material.

1 a I chose this material for the support platform because:

____

____

____

____

b I would also choose this material for: ______________________

2 a I chose this material for the crane because:

____

____

____

____

b I would also choose this material for: ______________________

3 a I chose this material for the plank because:

____

____

____

____

b I would also choose this material for: ______________________

Task 2

Testing the strength of concrete beams

Concrete is made by mixing sand and cement.
Louise and Brad wanted to find out which mixture made the strongest concrete beam.
They made some beams using different amounts of sand and cement.

1 What other material should they add to the sand and cement to make concrete?

____

2 Is the change to these materials reversible or irreversible?

____

3 Explain your answer.

____

____

____

____

A week after making the beams, they tested them to see how strong they were. From each beam they hung different masses, gradually increasing the mass until the beam broke.

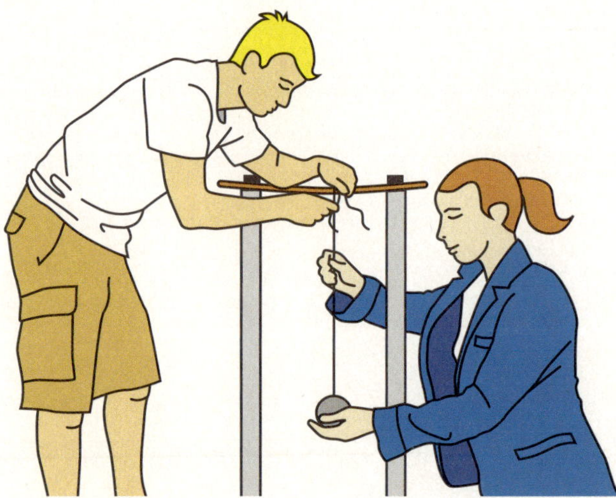

4 Describe one thing that they should do to make sure their experiment is safe.

____

____

____

____

Here is a table of their results:

measures of cement	measures of sand	mass at which beam broke (kg)
5	1	6.0
4	2	5.5
3	3	4.5
2	4	3.0

5 What effect does using more cement in the mixture have on the strength of the beam?

____

The children used their data to plot a graph.

6 On the grid below, plot a graph of the results from the table in an appropriate way.

7 What mass do you think will be needed to break the beam if 1 part cement and 5 parts sand are used?

____

8 Explain your answer.

____

____

____

____

Rocks and soils

Task 1 Natural or manufactured?

Read the text below. Underline in red all the words for types of natural rock. Underline in blue all the words for types of manufactured rock.

If you look around your environment you will see many different objects made from natural or manufactured materials. You might see slate roofs or roofs made of tiles. Buildings may have walls of bricks made from clay. Limestone, flint and granite are also used to make walls. Sometimes the walls might be covered with painted concrete or even marble. The glass in windows comes from sand and other chemicals. Lead may have been used to decorate the windows, and the frames may be made of wood, plastic or aluminium.

Task 2 Different rocks

A

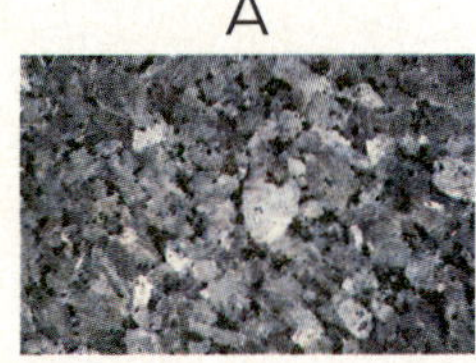

B

C

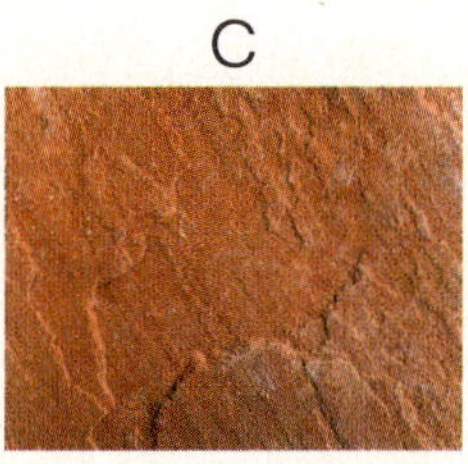

D

E

Children examined five different rocks of the same size.
Here is what they wrote about each rock:

Rock A has crystals which are about 5mm across. The crystals are white and brown and pink. There are some shiny crystals in the rock.
Rock B is whitish-grey. It is made of tiny grains and has some fossils of shells in it.
Rock C is light brown. It is made of tiny grains which look like sand.
Rock D is light grey and has lots of air bubbles in it. When it was put in water it floated.
Rock E is dark grey. We couldn't see separate grains. The piece of rock is quite thin.

1 Draw a line from the letter of each rock to its correct name.

Rock A	pumice
Rock B	slate
Rock C	granite
Rock D	limestone
Rock E	sandstone

2 Which scientific skill were the children using when they were examining the rocks?

____

Task 3 Different grains

Rocks that have been broken down by the wind and the rain become grains. Grains of different sizes are called by different names.

1 Read the text below. Underline in red all the words that name a size of grain.

> If the grains of a rock are so small that you can't see them on their own, that rock is called a mud. If you can just see separate grains, it is called a sand. Sands feel gritty between your fingers and toes. Granules are larger than sand grains but smaller than pebbles. Anything between a pea and a cricket ball in size is called a pebble. Cobbles are between a cricket ball and a football in size. Anything larger than a football is called a boulder.

2 Write down the different grain sizes mentioned above, from largest to smallest.

Largest: ____________________

____

____

____

____

Smallest: ____________________

3 With your partner, think of some common grainy rocks and decide which type of grain they usually have. Write down one example.

____

Task 4

Soil-sample experiment

Raj and Sally wanted to find out what percentage of humus, sand, gravel and pebbles were present in a sample of soil. They put some soil and water in a large coffee jar, shook it up and left it overnight.

Humus is the part of
soil that has decayed from
plants and animals.

1 How would this help Raj and Sally to find out the percentage of each material?

____

____

2 What safety precautions should they take when working with soil?

____

____

3 Draw a diagram to help explain what the children might observe.

4 Explain why they should repeat their test.

____

____

Task 5

Types of soil

Raj and Sally wanted to compare how permeable clay and sandy soil were.

1 What does 'permeable' mean?

____

They could use the following equipment:

- funnels
- coffee filters
- measuring cylinder
- weighing scales

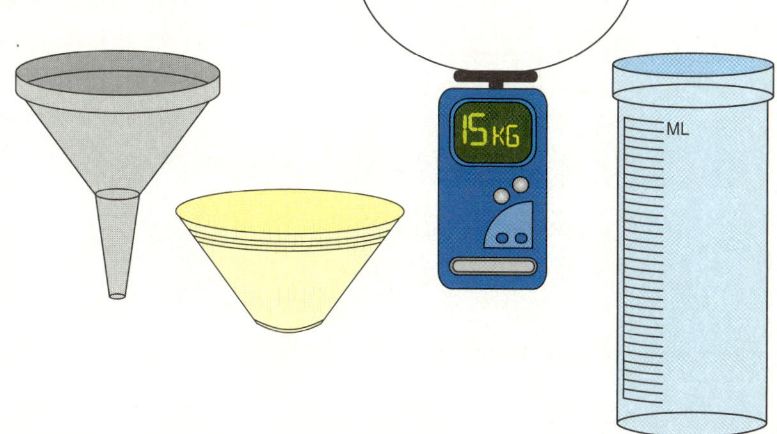

2 Predict what they would find out. Explain your prediction.

____

____

____

____

3 Write instructions for Sally and Raj.

____

____

____

____

4 List two factors they would need to keep the same to make sure their test was fair.

______________________________ ______________________________

5 What measurements will they need to take?

____

6 If your prediction is correct, what results should they expect to get?

____

____

____

____

Conductors and insulators

Task 1 Thermometers

Adam and Luba measured the temperature at various places using an alcohol thermometer.

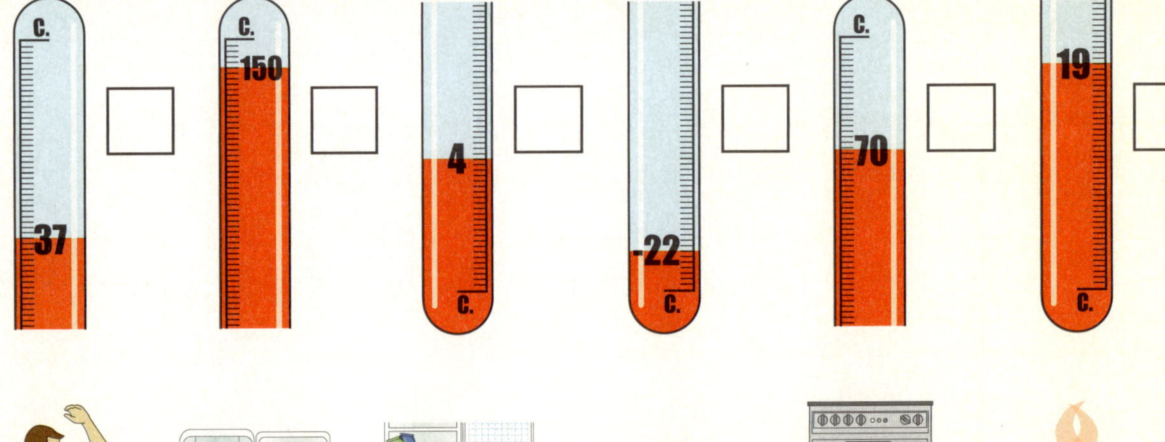

underarm

fridge

freezer

classroom

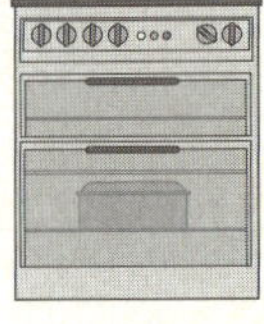
oven

hot soup

1 Read the temperature of each thermometer and write it in the box provided.

2 Which temperature is the lowest? ____________

3 Draw a line from each thermometer to the picture of where you think it measured the temperature.

Task 2 Insulators

Remember: a good conductor is a poor insulator, and a poor insulator is a good conductor.

Adam and Luba sorted a range of materials into good and poor thermal insulators. They recorded their work in a table, but forgot to label the columns.

1 Write an appropriate heading at the top of each column.

wood	steel
feathers	copper
fur	aluminium
	tin
	iron

2 Write two other materials that might go in the empty table cells.

Task 3

Adam's experiment

Adam set up the following investigation. He took five rods, made of different materials, and put a small piece of margarine on the end of each. He put the rods into a beaker of hot water. He timed how long it took the margarine to melt.

Here are his results:

iron	67 s
aluminium	42 s
wood	(did not melt)
plastic	2 min 30 s
glass	1 min 45 s

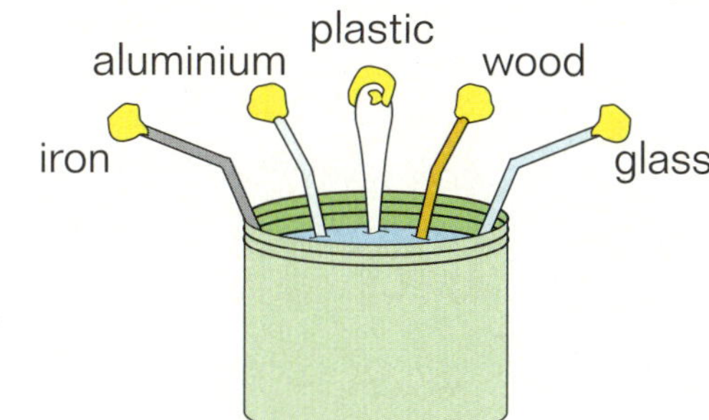

1 Why did the margarine on the wooden rod not melt while that on the iron rod did?

____

2 Explain the rest of Adam's results.

____

Adam put each rod in turn into an electric circuit with a lightbulb.

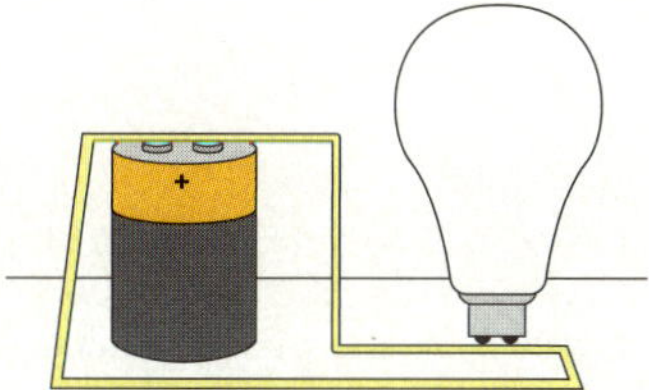

3 Complete the table to show what you think happened to the lightbulb.

Material	What happened to lightbulb
iron	
aluminium	
wood	
plastic	
glass	

4 Explain how you decided on your answers. What do you notice about the materials that were good thermal conductors?

____

One cold winter morning, Adam went outside and touched some metal railings, a window pane, and a tree trunk. 'That's funny,' he said, 'they're all at different temperatures.' Luba replied: 'They can't be: they're all as cold as each other.'

5 Who is correct? ____________

6 Explain your answer.

____

____

Task 4

Hot soup

Luba was going on a bike ride and wanted to take some hot soup for lunch. She wanted to find the best material to wrap around her container to keep the soup warm. She wrapped layers of several different materials – newspaper, cotton wool, bubble wrap and aluminium foil – around separate cans of hot water. She used a temperature sensor with a data logger to help her to record her results.

1 List two things Luba would need to do to make sure her test was fair.

____

____

____

____

The graph below shows Luba's results.

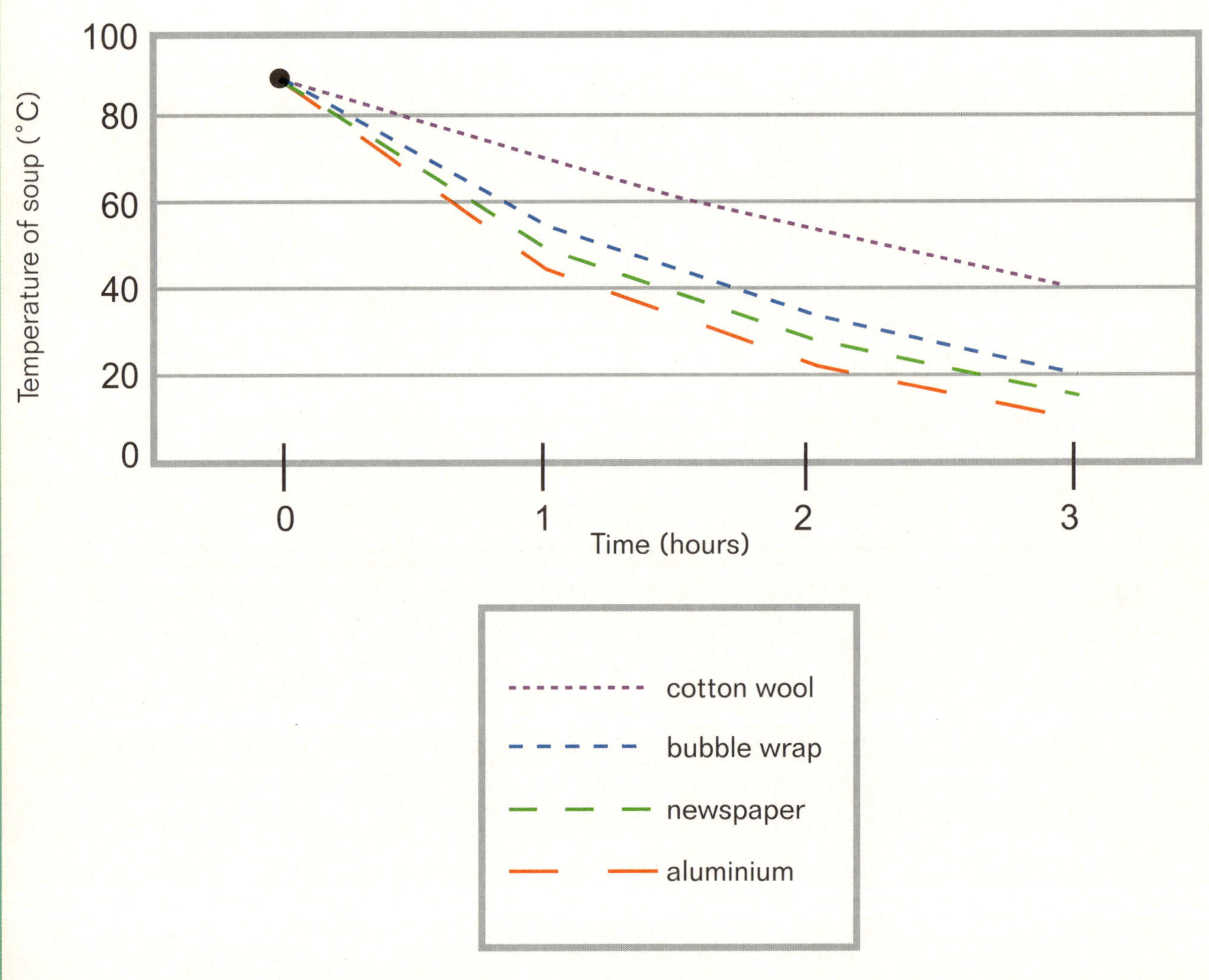

2 Which two materials are the best at keeping the soup warm?

____________________ ____________________

3 Why do you think they are good insulators?

4 The following summer, Luba was planning to go on a bike ride.
She wanted to keep her water bottle as cool as possible.
Which one of the materials she tested should she wrap around her bottle?

Remember: the same materials keep cold objects cold as keep warm objects warm.

5 What other situations can you think of when it is important to keep things warm?
What other situations can you think of when it is important to keep things cool?
Discuss these with your partner and write down one example of each.

Properties of materials

Task 1

This is the house that Jack built

When Jack built his house he used many different materials.
Each material was used because of its special properties.

In each box, write one material that Jack could have used for the object indicated, and name one property of the material that makes it good to use for that object.

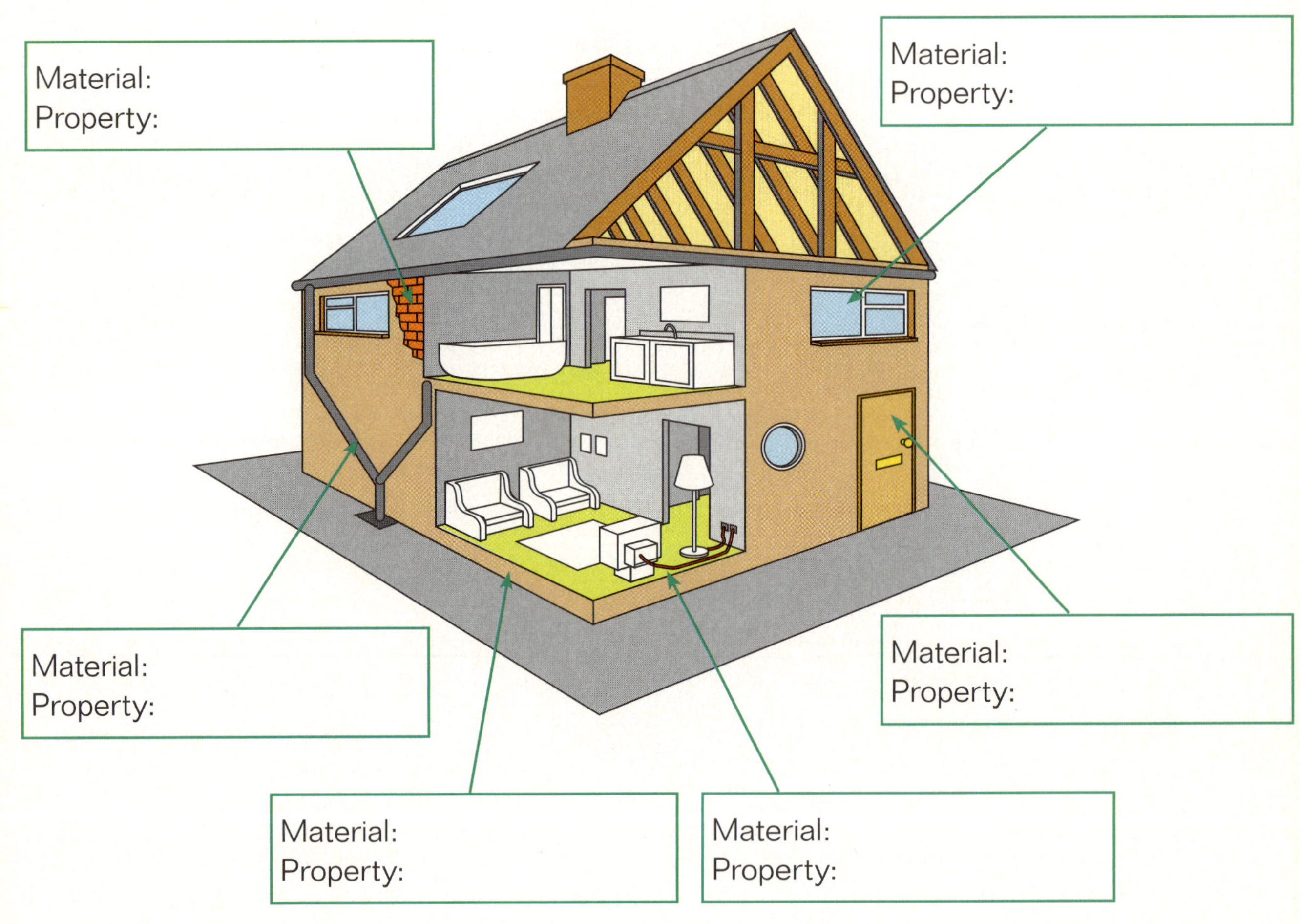

Task 2

Properties

For each property listed below, name one material having that property that Jack might have used in his house, and state where he might have used it.

Property	Material	Where this might be needed
hard		
transparent		
solid		
flexible		

Property	Material	Where this might be needed
shiny		
malleable		
magnetic		
able to conduct electricity		

Task 3

Which material?

Samina and Darren wanted to find the best material for the kitchen worktop in Jack's house. The materials they tested were:

- cork tile
- granite
- melamine
- wood
- ceramic tile

They tested the materials to find which was the most scratchproof. Here are some of their observations:

> A piece of wood scratched the cork tile.
> Granite scratched melamine.
> A ceramic tile scratched the melamine but not the granite.
> Melamine scratched the wood.

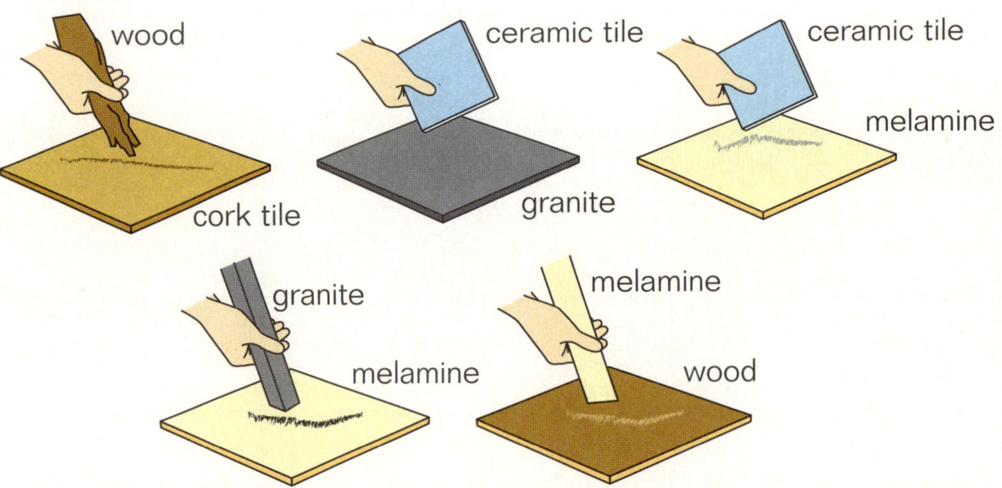

1 Describe how they could have done the experiment to make sure it was a fair test.

____

____

____

____

2 List the materials in order from most to least scratchproof.

______________ most scratchproof

____

____

____

______________ least scratchproof

3 Which of the materials is the hardest?

____

4 Explain your answer.

____

____

____

5 a Name another property that a kitchen work surface should have.

____

Now think about how you would test materials to find out if they have this property.

b What factor would you keep the same?

____

c What factor would you change?

____

d What factor would you measure?

____

Remember: the hardest material is the one that can't be scratched by any of the others.

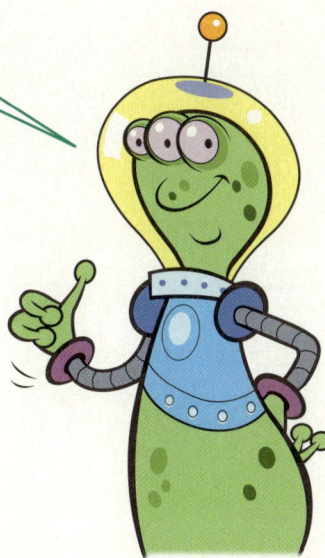

Reversible and irreversible changes

Task 1

Describing changes

Explain the difference between a reversible and an irreversible change.

____

____

____

____

Remember: in an irreversible change, a new substance is formed.

Task 2

Reversible or irreversible?

1 Look at the list of changes below.

Underline in red the changes that are reversible, and explain how you know.
Underline in blue the changes that are irreversible, and explain how you know.

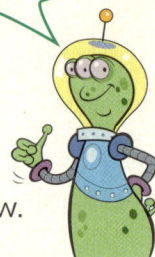

a *Adding water to cement.* This change is ________________ because:

____

b *Adding water to salt.* This change is ________________ because:

____

c *Adding water to plaster of Paris.* This change is ________________ because:

____

d *Adding water to oil.* This change is ________________ because:

____

e *Adding water to glass beads.* This change is ________________ because:

____

f *Adding water to jelly mix.* This change is ________________ because:

____

g *Adding water to soil.* This change is ________________ because:

____

2 Think of some other examples of materials added to water, and decide whether the changes are reversible or irreversible.

____

____

Task 3

Catching fire

Some materials are combustible. This means they are capable of burning.

1 What gas is needed for a material to burn? ______________

2 Where does this gas usually come from? ______________

3 What two gases are produced when a wax candle burns?

______________ ______________

4 Tick those of the pictures below that show combustible materials.

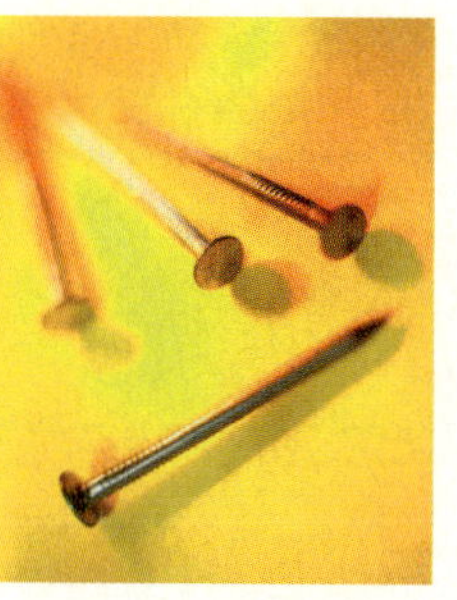

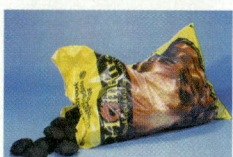

5 Explain why a candle doesn't burn unless it is lit by a match.

____

____

6 Here is a picture of a candle snuffer, which is used to put out a candle. Explain how the snuffer works.

____

____

____

____

7 Write one similarity between rusting and burning.

____

8 Write one difference between rusting and burning.

____

Remember the 'fire triangle': fuel, heat, oxygen.

Task 4

Does it stay the same?

Look at each of the following changes.
For each change, decide whether any new materials are made.
If so, write their names or describe them.

Change	Is a new material made?	Changes into ...?
composting vegetables, grass and leaves		
burning petrol		
grating cheese		
adding vinegar to sodium bicarbonate		
leaving a nail in water for a day		
drying washing on the line		
adding yeast to sugar and water		
heating a mixture of sugar and water		
heating egg whites		
stretching a plastic bag		

Task 5 Baking

When we bake bread or cakes we sometimes use a raising agent (either a mixture of sugar, yeast and water, or baking powder). Explain what the raising agent does.

____

____

____

____

Task 6 Dissolving

1 Complete the following sentence:

When a solid dissolves in a liquid, a ______________ is formed.

2 Tick the substances below that you predict will be soluble in water.

sugar **pepper** **citric acid** **washing soda** **flour** **salt** **plaster of Paris**

cement **custard powder** **instant coffee granules** **yeast** **talcum powder**

3 How could you test your predictions?

____

____

____

____

4 What would you expect to observe if your predictions are correct?

____

____

____

5 What could you measure to compare the solubility of different substances?

____

____

____

6 How would you make sure your tests are carried out safely?

____

____

Mixing and separating materials

Task 1 Separating mixtures

Listed on the left are some mixtures, and on the right are four ways of separating mixtures.

Draw a line from each mixture to the easiest way of separating it.

salt water	filtering
iron and sand	
sand and water	
water and sugar	using a magnet
brass and steel screws	
dried beans and lentils	
sunflower seeds and cress seeds	evaporating the liquid
chalky water	
talcum powder and water	
steel cans and aluminium cans	sieving

Task 2 Which mixture?

Work with your partner to complete this task.

1 Write one other mixture that could be separated by filtering:

____

2 Write one other mixture that could be separated by using a magnet:

____

3 Write one other mixture that could be separated by evaporating the liquid:

____

4 Write one other mixture that could be separated by sieving:

____

5 Join with another pair and ask them how they would separate your mixtures. Record any new ideas below.

____

____

____

____

Task 3 Sieving stones and soil

Priya and Jack wanted to separate a mixture of stones and soil.
They had four different things to use as sieves:

a piece of a pair of tights

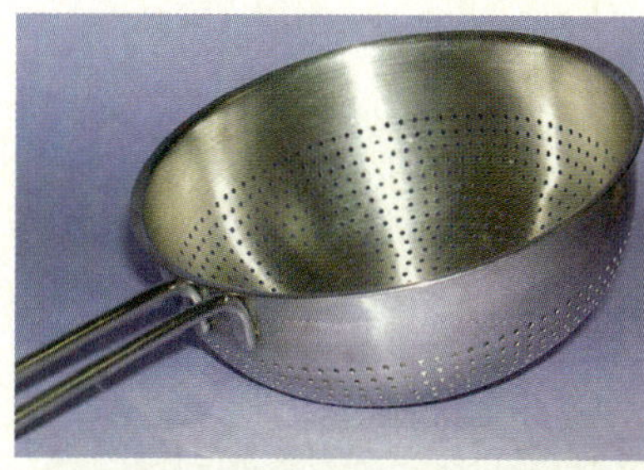

a flour sieve

a tea strainer

stone sieves

1 Priya said they should try to separate out the largest grains first.
Jack thought they should use each sieve in turn.
Write down the order in which they should use the sieves.

____

2 Explain your answer.

____

____

____

Task 4 Drinking seawater

In some parts of the world where there is very little rainfall, people use seawater to provide them with pure drinking water.

1 Explain how 'pure' water is different from seawater.

____

____

2 What do you think needs to be done to the seawater to make it suitable for drinking?

____

____

____

____

Task 5

Dissolving sugar and water

Shaun and Anna put a teaspoonful of icing sugar into 100 cm^3 of water and stirred the mixture. They then added more teaspoonfuls, stirring until no more sugar would dissolve. They recorded the number of teaspoonfuls of icing sugar that they had added.

They then repeated the test with different kinds of sugar:
- castor
- granulated
- brown
- muscovado

1 What do you think they were trying to find out? Tick the correct box.

which sugar is most soluble in water ☐

whether stirring affects how much sugar dissolves ☐

which sugar makes the clearest solution ☐

which sugar is most soluble in water ☐

how to prepare a mixture of sugar and water ☐

2 Explain your answer.

___

___

___

Here is a table of their results:

Sugar type	Number of teaspoonfuls dissolved in water
icing	4
castor	6
granulated	4
brown	3
muscovado	2

They were asked to draw a graph of their results.

3 Which of the following is the best type of graph to draw?

pie chart ☐

line graph ☐

bar chart ☐

4 Explain your answer.

____

____

____

Shaun said that castor sugar was the best sugar.

5 Why do you think he said that?

____

____

6 Explain why you do or do not agree with Shaun.

____

____

____

7 How could Shaun and Anna improve their investigation?

____

____

____

8 They wanted to get back the sugars from the solutions, so they put them on the window sill and left them for a week.

Why did they do this?

____

____

____

Solids, liquids and gases

Task 1 Solids

1 Amy and Bradley observed some solids and recorded their observations. Tick the observations that are true for **all** solids.

has a fixed shape	☐	is slippery	☐
is slimy	☐	cannot be poured	☐
is shiny	☐	is hard	☐
is opaque	☐	is cold	☐
conducts electricity	☐	can be squashed	☐

2 Put a circle around all the materials below that are usually solid.

chewing gum **vinegar** **clay** **wood** **tomato ketchup**

candle wax **salt** **sand** **plastic** **petrol** **sponge**

3 Write one thing that all solids have in common.

____

4 Look at the pictures and tick all the objects that contain a gas.

helium balloon

bottle of milk

fizzy drink

cake

butane container

empty bottle

jelly

butter

can of oil

synthetic sponge

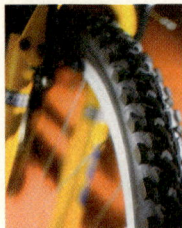

bicycle tyre

granite

biscuit

5 List four other objects that contain a gas.

____

6 Write one thing that all gases have in common.

____

Task 2

Differences between solid, liquid and gas

1 Draw lines from each state of matter to the correct descriptions of it.

solid	can flow
	fills the bottom of a container
	can easily be changed in size and shape
liquid	is rigid
	can easily be squashed
	keeps its shape and size
gas	can be held in your hand
	keeps its size but not its shape

2 Amy said that all gases had a smell.

Is she correct? ______________

Explain your answer.

____

____

____

3 Bradley said that all liquids were see-through.

Is he correct? ______________

Explain your answer.

____

____

____

4 Ikrit said that solids are always heavier than gases.

Is he correct? ______________

Explain your answer.

____

____

____

Task 3

Light as air

Iwan said that a balloon full of air would weigh the same as a balloon with no air in.

What activity could you do to show Iwan that an inflated balloon weighs more than a balloon with no air? You can draw a picture to help you explain.

Task 4

Squeezing a sponge

Henry told Alice it was nearly impossible to change the size of a solid by squashing it.

Alice told Henry it could be very easy if you chose the right material.

Explain why both children were correct for certain sorts of solids.

Task 5 Air

Air is a mixture of gases. Clean dry air contains approximately:

- 78 % nitrogen
- 0.03 % carbon dioxide
- 21 % oxygen
- 1 % other gases

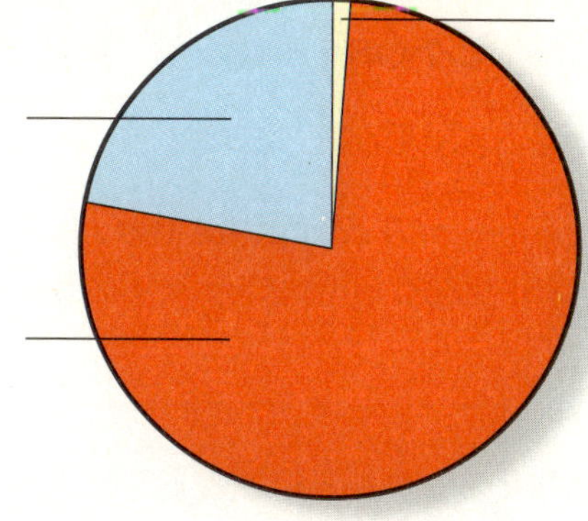

1 Label the pie chart to show the proportions of different gases in the air.

2 Which gas is not shown on the pie chart? Explain why.

____

____

____

Task 6 Smelling roses

Alice and Henry walked into a room and could smell the roses that they could see at the other side of the room.

Explain why they could smell the roses.

____

____

____

____

____

____

____

Changing state

Task 1

Crossword

Materials can change state in certain conditions.

Read the clues below and complete the crossword.
All the answers are to do with liquids, solids, gases, and changing state.

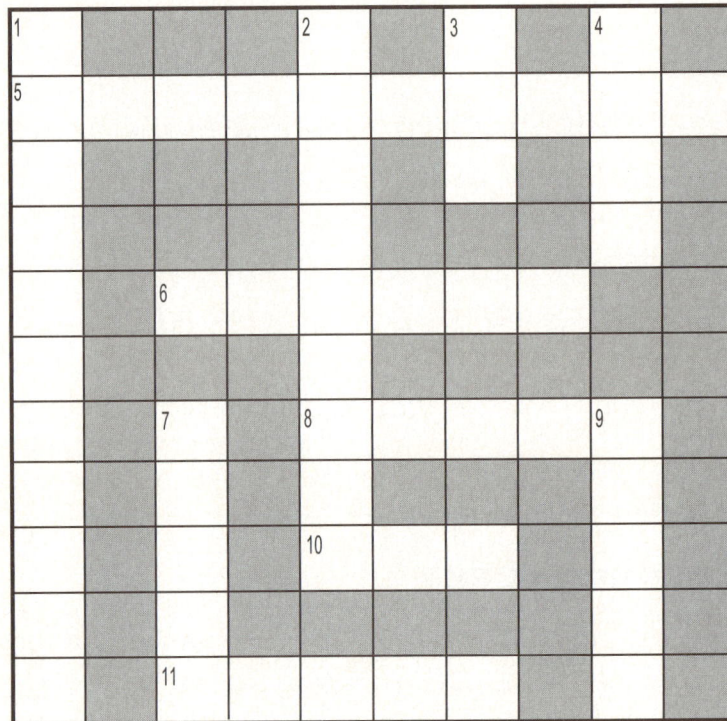

1				2		3		4	
5									
		6							
		7		8				9	
				10					
		11							

Across

5 When water seems to disappear into the air, it …. (10 letters)

6 Change a liquid to a solid. (6 letters)

8 Tiny droplets of very hot water suspended in the air. (5 letters)

10 The … helps water outside to evaporate. (3 letters)

11 The state to which a liquid changes when it freezes. (5 letters)

Down

1 A measure of how hot or cold something is. (11 letters)

2 When a gas turns into a liquid, it …. (9 letters)

3 One of the three states of matter. (3 letters)

4 To change a liquid into a gas, this is needed. (4 letters)

7 As a heated liquid turns into a gas, it …. (5 letters)

9 When a solid turns into a liquid, it …. (5 letters)

Task 2 Explanations

For each question below, write a full explanation of your answer.

1 How are boiling and evaporating similar?

____

____

2 What is the difference between melting and freezing?

____

____

3 What is the difference between heating and boiling?

____

____

Task 3 Changes of state

1 Underneath each picture, write the name of the process that is happening in it.

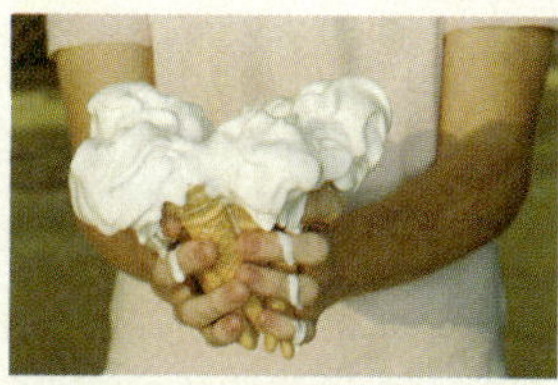

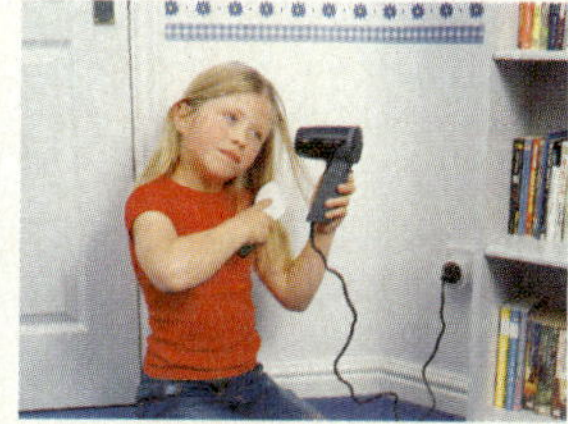

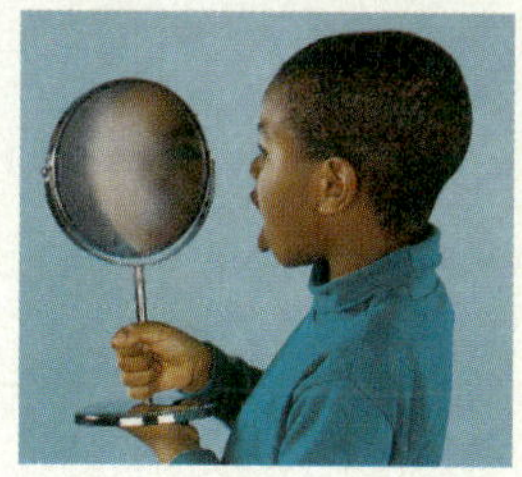

2 With your partner, think of other examples of changes of state. Write one down.

____

____

Task 4 Water cycle

Look at this diagram of the water cycle.

1 List three different places on the diagram where evaporation is taking place.

____

____

____

2 Write one place where condensation is taking place.

____

3 Make a list of things that might happen to rain that falls on the grass.

____

____

____

____

____

____

Task 5 States of water

Sam's teacher set up some equipment so that she could tell her class about the different states of water.

She asked the children to draw and label a diagram to show changes and states of water.

Here is what one child labelled:

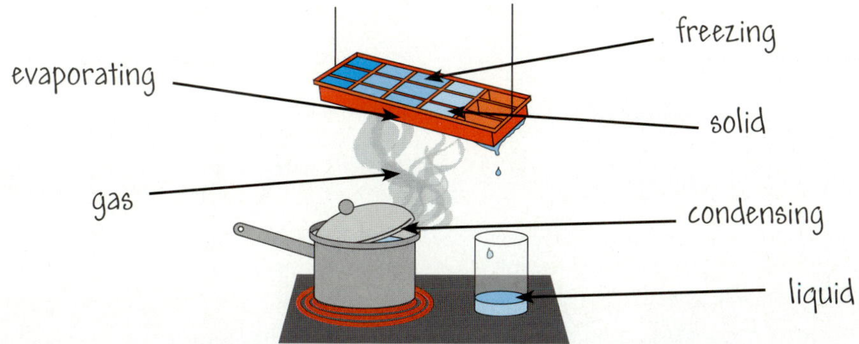

1 Put a tick next to each correct label and a cross next to each incorrect label.

Sam predicted that if 150 g of water evaporated from the saucepan then 150 g of water would be collected in the beaker.

She recorded the mass of water that escaped from the saucepan and the mass that she collected in the beaker. Here are her results:

water that escaped from the saucepan: 150 g
water collected in the beaker: 57 g

2 Explain why the two measurements are not the same.

____

____

3 Why did the tray above the saucepan contain ice?

____

____

4 What precautions must be taken to make sure the activity is carried out safely?

____

____

Sc4 Physical processes

Electricity

Task 1 Correcting circuits

Look at the picture of the electrical circuit that Parveen and David have made.
They used an electrical symbol for one component in their picture, and realistic drawings for the other components.

Read their description with a partner and discuss how you would correct the writing and drawing. Then cross out and correct the parts that are wrong.

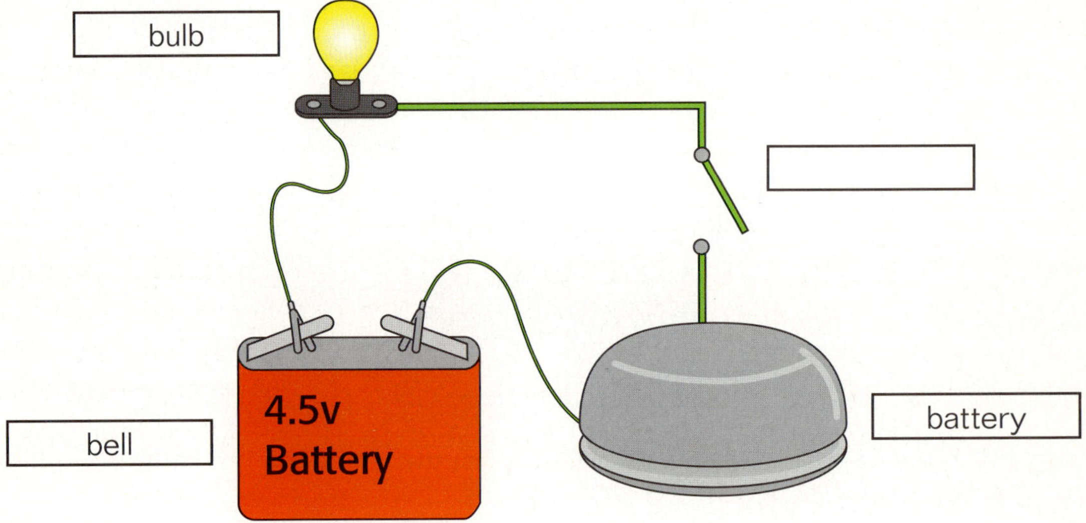

We used a 3-volt battery, which is really 4 electrical cells in cardboard packaging. We connected some wire that was completely covered in brightly coloured plastic to the knife terminals on the battery. This plastic is a really good conductor and makes sure the electricity gets round the circuit. Then we connected the battery to a bulb and a switch. We also put a motor in the circuit. One wire from it was connected to the battery and another wire went from the bell to the switch. The picture we have drawn shows what you must do to make the bell and bulb work.

Task 2

How a lightbulb works

1 Read the following passage.

Mr Wales showed Class 6 a torch bulb. He explained that the glass on a torch bulb is transparent so that it lets the light through when it is switched on and also so that you can see inside it. If the glass were only translucent, light would pass through it when the bulb was switched on but you would not be able to see what the bulb was made of. Mr Wales explained that there are two vertical wire filaments supporting a much thinner wire filament which links the two vertical wires. We could see a blob of glass: a very small bead that helped to keep these wires upright. But we could not see where the wires came from. The metal screw case at the bottom of the bulb hid where the wires went to. Mr Wales told us to look carefully at the bottom of the bulb. This was made of black plastic with a bead of metal in the middle. Inside the metal case, one of the filaments went from the metal bead and passed into the top of the light bulb. The other filament was attached to the inside of the metal case. When the metal bead was placed on the knife terminal of a 4.5 V battery and the metal case was placed on the other battery terminal, the bulb lit. This was because there was now a complete electric circuit. The electric current went up a vertical filament and then into the much thinner filament. This bit of filament has a higher resistance, and as it tries to stop the current passing it becomes white-hot, making light.

2 Working with a discussion partner, mark the text as follows:

- **a** Underline in pencil a property of glass.
- **b** Circle in pencil the structures that support the finer piece of wire.
- **c** Underline in red crayon what helps to keep the vertical filaments in place.
- **d** Circle in red crayon what is on the bottom of the bulb.
- **e** Underline in blue crayon where the filaments are in the metal-screw part of the bulb.
- **f** Circle in blue crayon what makes the bulb give out light.

3 Use your text marking to label and annotate this diagram of a torch bulb:

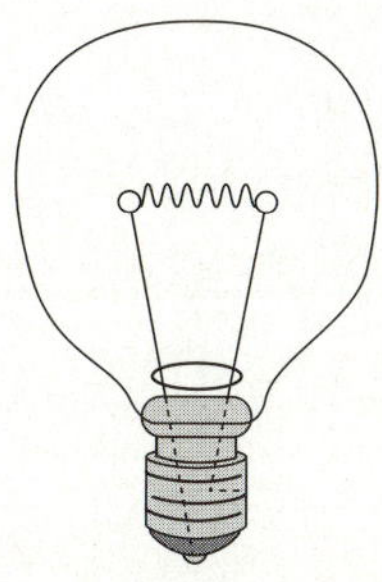

Task 3

Model lighthouse and foghorn

Thomas and Bryn made a model lighthouse with a foghorn. They used a transparent plastic bottle, plastic-covered wires, a bulb and bulb holder, a 4.5-volt battery, and a buzzer for the foghorn. They wanted the light and buzzer to work only when the circuit was closed. They used a piece of wood with two nails so that they could experiment with making a switch and find out which materials would be good at switching their circuit on and off.

1 **a** Draw a picture of what you think Thomas and Bryn's circuit looked like.

b Check your answer and make adjustments if necessary.

2 Draw a circuit diagram based on the picture you have drawn. Label each component.

To make their lighthouse and buzzer work, they tried a variety of objects made from different materials. They held these objects across the gap between the two nails, observed what happened, and recorded their answers in a table.

They used:

- metal scissors
- a plastic pen
- a metal teaspoon
- a plastic teaspoon
- a wooden ruler
- an aluminium bun case.

3 Complete the two-column table below, including the headings, to show what should have happened in Thomas and Bryn's experiment.

4 What do you think they noticed about the objects that made the bulb and buzzer work?

____

____

____

5 What is the scientific name for a material that lets electricity through?

____

6 What is the scientific name for a material that does not let electricity through?

____

7 Name two materials that Thomas and Bryn could use to stop the flow of electricity.

____

____

Sc4 Physical processes

Task 4 Brighter lights

Thomas worked with Molly to find out how changing the number of electrical cells in a circuit could affect how bright a bulb was.

They could use up to three 1.5 volt cells with battery boxes, wires with crocodile clips all made the same length and of the same material, one torch bulb and bulb holder, and a switch.

1 With a partner, discuss what you think Thomas and Molly should do.
Complete the planning framework below.

Question for investigation:

'When we change the ________________, what will happen to the ________________?'

We will change: ________________________________

We will observe and judge: ________________________________

We will keep these things the same to make the test fair:

____

2 Draw a diagram of their experiment.

Task 5 Even brighter lights

Thomas remembered that they had used a light sensor to measure how much light is produced. He designed an investigation to measure how much light was given off when different numbers of electrical cells were used. He drew his design, but did not label it.

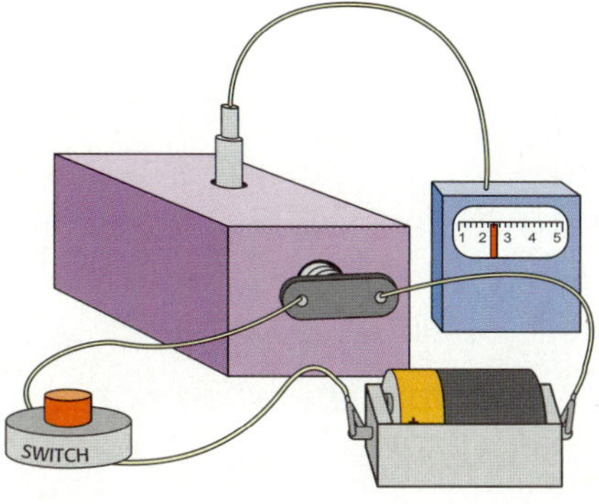

Remember: always use the first column for the factor that is being changed and the second column for the factor that is being measured.

1 Look at his design and label it.

2 He recorded his results in a table, but forgot to put the headings on. Complete it for him, and then write what the experiment discovered.

one	2
two	4
three	6

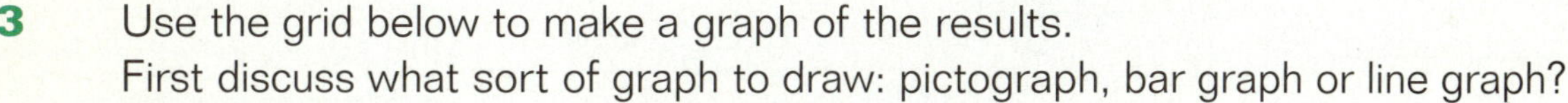

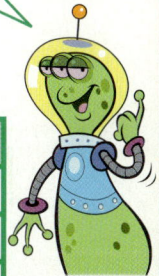

3 Use the grid below to make a graph of the results.
First discuss what sort of graph to draw: pictograph, bar graph or line graph?

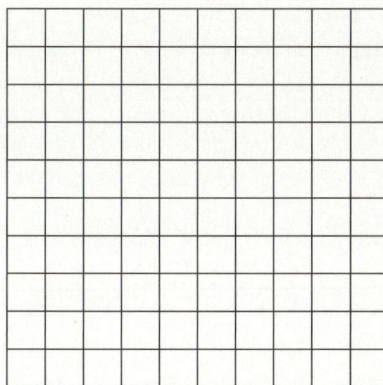

4 Write what you decided to do, and why, and what you found out.

Task 1 The eyes have it

We need light in order to see. If you went into a cave or mine or underground dungeon and the lights were out you would be in complete darkness. You would not be able to see anything because there would be no light to enter the eye.

Look at the picture of an eye below. In order to see, we have to let light enter the eye. Light enters through what looks like a black hole, the pupil, in the centre of the eye. It is surrounded by the coloured iris. The pupil can change its size. When it is dull or dark, it grows to let as much light as possible in through the pupil. The white of the eye is tough and helps to hold the eye in place. Eyebrows and eyelashes help to stop dirt and dust entering the eye and damaging it.

Discuss the picture of the eye with your partner. Label it by writing the name of each part in the box provided.

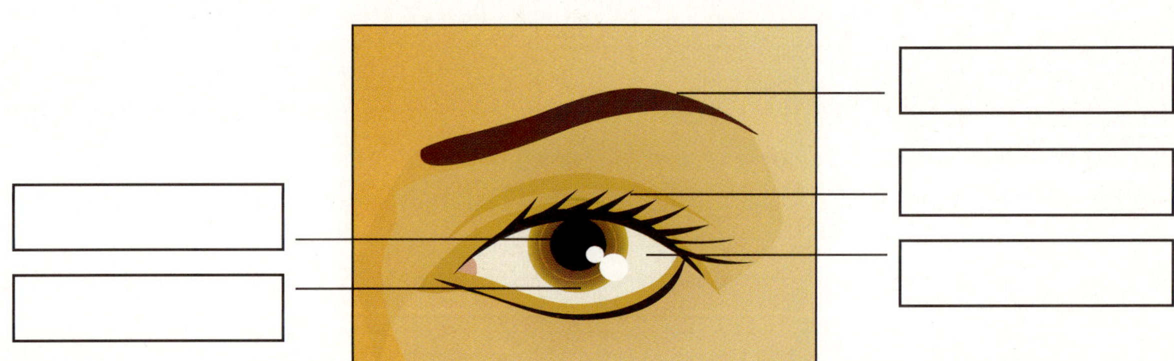

Task 2

How we see objects

We see an object when light enters the eye from it. Light first has to shine onto the object. When we look at the object the light is reflected from it into our eye.

Look at the picture of the fruit in the bowl on the table in this room. The curtains are drawn. The light source is the electric light hanging from the ceiling. Use lines with arrows to show how light travels so that the person sees the fruit.

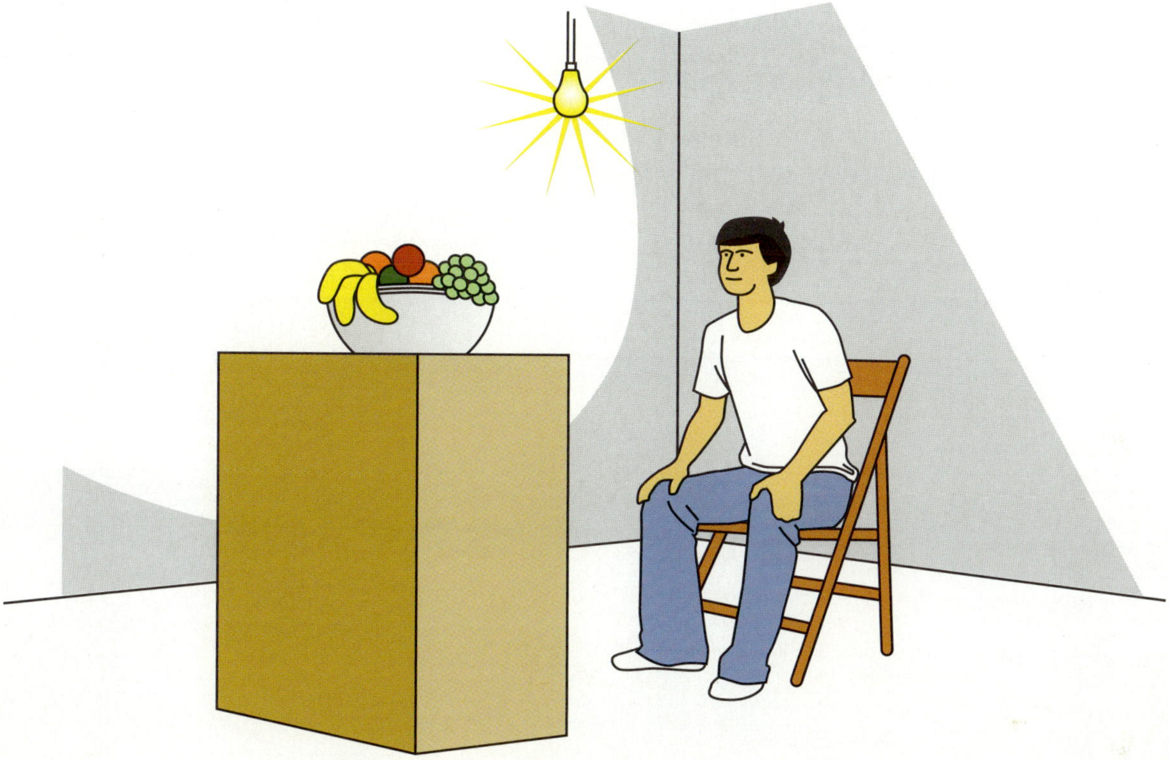

Remember to use a ruler to draw the rays of light: light always travels in straight lines from sources and reflecting surfaces.

Task 3 Shadows

Abdul wanted to investigate what happens to the length of an object's shadow when the distance of the object from a torch changes.

1 Which one of these materials should he use for the object casting the shadow? Tick one of them.

- clear plastic ☐
- thick card ☐
- thin tissue paper ☐
- net-curtain fabric ☐

2 Explain the reason for your choice using these words: *transparent*, *translucent*, *opaque*.

____

____

____

____

____

____

Task 4

Shadow experiment

Abdul wanted to investigate shadows. He decided to shine a torch horizontally at a solid disc in a dark room, and measure the diameter of the shadow cast by the disc on the wall when the torch was held at different distances from the disc. He predicted that when the disc was near to the light source, the shadow would be small. He shone the torch from five different places, recording his results in a table.

1 What factor is Abdul changing?

____

2 What factor is he measuring?

____

3 What factors does he need to keep the same to make his test fair?

____

4 Abdul recorded his results in a table, but forgot to put the headings on. Complete it for him. Remember to include the units.

5	12.0
10	11.5
15	10.0
20	9.5
25	9.0

5 Draw a graph of the results on the grid provided.

6 What pattern can you see in your graph?

____

____

____

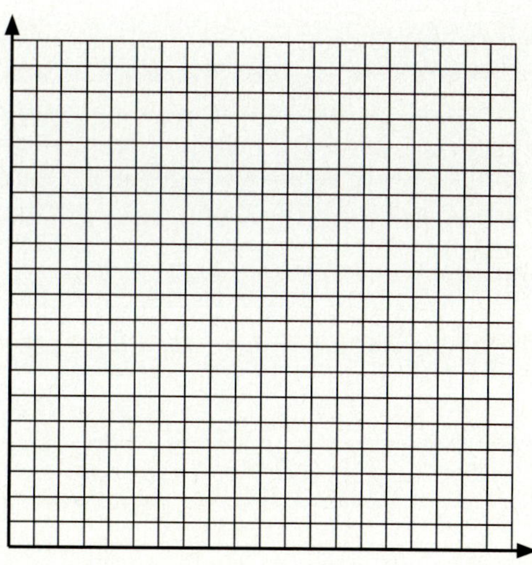

7 Was Abdul's prediction correct?

____

____

Sound

Task 1

Sound words

Read the passage below. Some important words are missing. Complete the passage using only words from this list. You can use words more than once. Not all the words are needed.

pitch loudness vibrate vibrations quiet noise sound tension loud plucked high low

The band were tuning their guitars. Each player adjusted the tension in the strings to get the right ________________. The tighter strings made ________________-pitched notes and the slacker strings made sounds of ________________ pitch. Pitch is measured by the number of ________________ per second. Sounds of ________________ pitch do not ________________ as frequently as ________________-pitched sounds. They plucked the strings hard so the noise was very ________________.

Task 2

Good vibrations

With a discussion partner, decide what a 'vibration' is and what 'pitch' means.
Then write down what you have decided.

A vibration is:

____

____

____

____

Pitch means:

____

____

____

____

Task 3

Investigation of hearing and sound

Jane tested some materials to see which was best at muffling sound. She compared the effects of pieces of foil, cotton wool and bubble wrap, all of the same size, wrapped around a battery-powered electric buzzer.

1 When the buzzer vibrates, how does the sound reach her brain? Complete the pathway by writing two things that have to vibrate before Jane hears the sound.

buzzer vibrates → ________ vibrates → ________ vibrates → Jane's brain gets the message

2 What could Jane use to measure the loudness of the sound from the buzzer? Draw a picture of the equipment and how you think Jane would do the test.

3 What else should Jane do to make sure the test was fair?

____

Jane recorded her results in a table like this:

Type of material	Loudness of sound
cotton wool	4
aluminium foil	12
bubble wrap	9

4 What sort of graph should Jane draw for these results? Why?

____

____

____

5 What should Jane conclude from her results?

____

____

____

Earth, Sun and Moon

Task 1

'Earth, Sun and Moon' quiz

Jon has forgotten a lot of facts about the Earth, the Sun and the Moon. Please help him! He has a set of descriptions and a set of words. Match each description with the correct word. You may use some words more than once.

Earth **night** **Earth day** **Sun** **daytime** **sunset**
sunrise **axis** **phases** **year** **Moon** **lunar month**

a spherical planet that orbits the Sun	
one rotation of the Earth on its axis in 24 hours	
when the Sun appears in the sky at the beginning of the day	
a hot spherical star	
when the Sun disappears from view at the end of the day	
the time taken for the Earth to orbit the Sun	
the period when a given part of Earth is facing the Sun	
a natural satellite of the Earth	
the time taken for the Moon to orbit the Earth	
the period when a given part of Earth is facing away from the Sun	
an imaginary line around which the Earth spins	
the changes in the appearance of the Moon as it orbits the Earth	

Task 2 Sun worshippers

Bob and Ali did some research into where the Sun would appear to be in the sky at midday on December 21 and June 21. They drew an outline of the buildings they could see from their south-facing classroom. They drew yellow circles to represent where the Sun rose in the morning and where it set in the evening.

1 Write what season it is in the UK on:

a 21 December ________________

b 21 June ________________

2 What safety precautions should they take while doing their experiment?

____

3 Where would the Sun be at midday on 21 December? Draw this in yellow and label the diagram. Draw arrows to show how the Sun appears to move during the day in December.

4 Where would the Sun be at midday on 21 June?
Draw and colour this red or orange on the diagram.

5 Add arrows to show how the Sun appears to move across the sky in June.

Task 3

Shadow length in Spring

On 21 March, Ali and Bob decided to investigate how the lengths of shadows changed during the day. They filled a plastic bucket with sand and stood a broom handle in it.
They measured the length of the shadow at different times of the day, and recorded their results in a table.

Time of day	Length of shadow (cm)
9 am	140
10 am	125
11 am	110
12 noon	100
1 pm	108
2 pm	
3 pm	138
4 pm	150

They forgot to measure the shadow at 2 pm.

They drew a graph of their results on a computer so that they could estimate the shadow length at 2 pm. Their graph is shown on the next page.

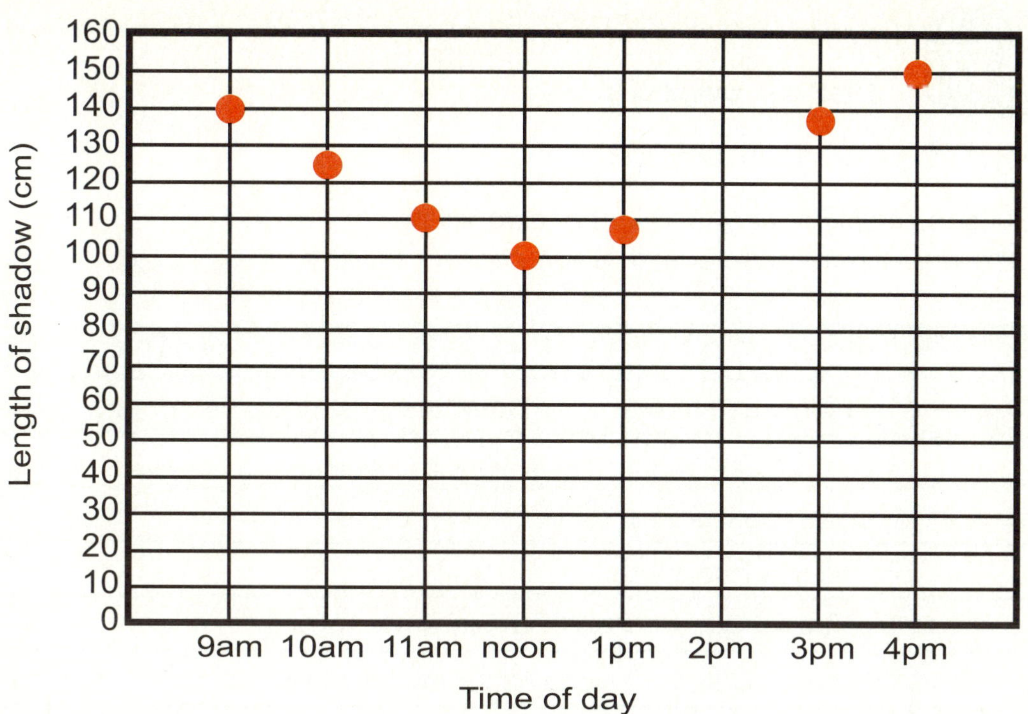

1 What is the length of the shadow at 2 pm?
Estimate the answer from the graph and add it to the table.

2 How did you find your answer?

____

____

3 Use the graph to predict the length of the shadow at these times:

a 9:30 am ______________

b 10:30 am ______________

c 12:30 am ______________

d 2 pm ______________

e 5 pm ______________

4 When is the shadow shortest? Why?

____

____

5 How would the shadow at 12 noon be different on 21 June?

____

____

Forces and movement

Task 1 Force words

This activity involves words about forces.

Use the clues to complete the words in the table below.
Then find the words in the word-search diagram.

Word	Clue
U_______	This force acts upwards on objects suspended in water or air.
F_______	The force that tends to stop things moving.
_____N	Force is measured in this unit.
S_____	Found in a forcemeter.
____	The force used to move things towards you.
____	The force used to move things away from you.
_____T	Made of iron or cobalt or nickel – it attracts some metals.
_______	This force pulls living things and objects towards the centre of the Earth.

U	G	R	A	V	I	T	Y	F	O
P	H	C	P	F	B	E	V	P	I
T	S	A	U	S	O	D	A	U	N
H	P	L	L	S	P	R	G	S	E
R	R	F	L	P	J	U	C	H	W
U	I	W	O	H	X	T	S	E	T
S	N	M	A	G	N	E	T	H	O
T	G	F	R	I	C	T	I	O	N
B	Z	G	H	P	A	O	W	F	D
A	L	T	G	E	B	J	M	O	I

Task 2

Magnets

Look at these diagrams of two disc magnets.

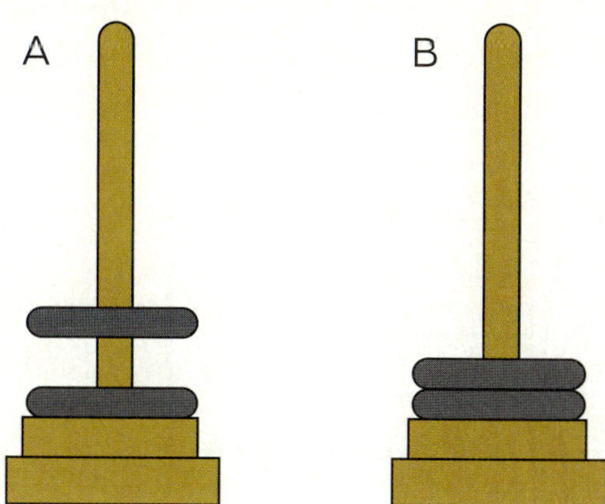

1 Why do the magnets in diagram A remain apart from each other while the magnets in diagram B appear to stick together? Annotate the diagrams and write an explanation below.

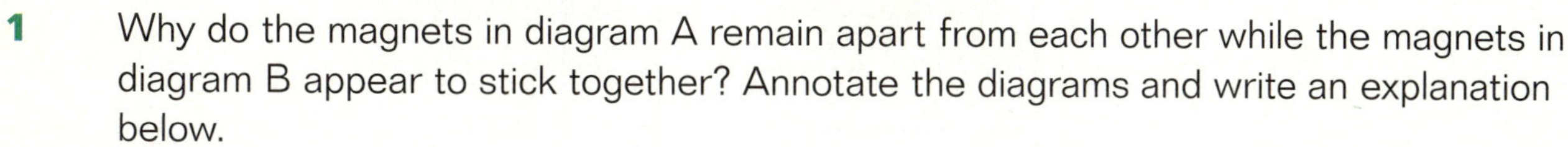

Amy has some plastic-covered magnetic marbles. There is a small magnet inside each one. She usually wins with these.

2 With a partner, draw and label a diagram to show why these marbles, when rolled, will usually stick to one another. Label the poles of the magnet in each marble.

3 Why are the marbles attracted to each other?

4 Name two other toys that make use of magnets.

Task 3

Magnet survey

In a survey of the classroom, Class 5 found that not all things were attracted to a bar magnet. They made a list of the things they tested and recorded whether or not each thing was attracted by a magnet. Complete the results table below. Put a tick if you think the object is magnetic and a cross if it you think it is not magnetic.

steel scissors	
plastic pen	
aluminium can	
steel can	
plastic paper clip	
brass pin	
iron nail	
copper wire	
gold ring	
10-pence coin	

Task 4

Magnet investigation

Miss Brown provided Year 6 with an iron bar magnet, small alnico magnets made of the metals nickel and cobalt, steel paper clips, steel ball bearings, a ruler, and digital scales.

alnico

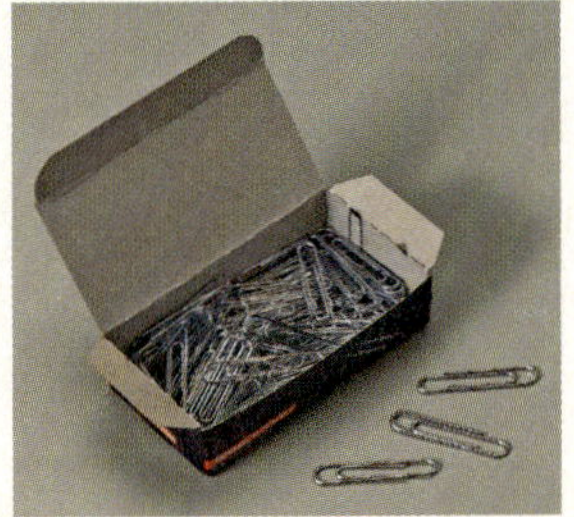

iron

The children had to plan an investigation to find out which magnet was the strongest, using any of the equipment that she had provided. Complete the planning chart below.

We want to find out which is the strongest: the iron bar magnet or the alnico magnet.

The factor we will change is: ______________________________

The factor we will measure is: ______________________________

We will keep these factors the same to make the test fair:

____

Task 5 Pushes and pulls

1 We use arrows to represent pushing and pulling forces. The length of an arrow represents how strong the force is, and the direction of the arrow represents the direction of the force. Discuss the pictures below and then add arrows to each picture to show the relative sizes and directions of the forces. Remember that gravity is an invisible force that pulls objects towards the centre of the Earth.

dropping a football

sailing boat moving forwards

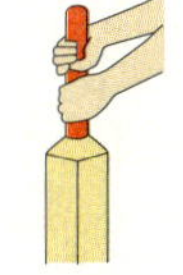
lifting a cricket bat

pulling a toy train

2 Alison put an inflated balloon in a tank of water. She pushed it down and held it under the water. When she let go it was pushed up to the surface by the upward force of the water – upthrust.
Add arrows to the three pictures to show what happened and how the forces acted on the balloon.

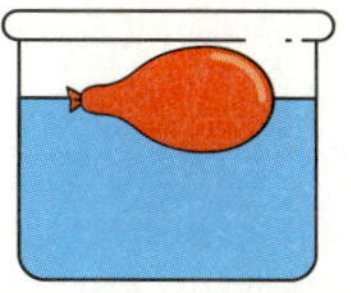
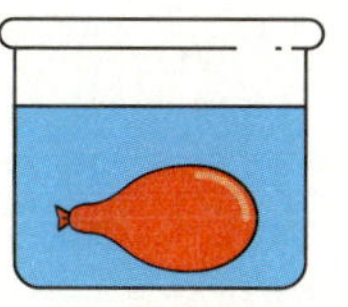
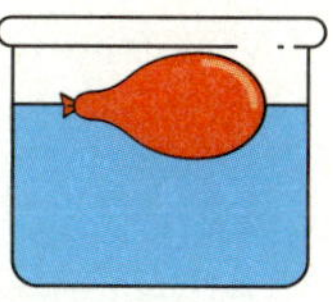

3 Jack and Katy hung a stone on a forcemeter and weighed it. Then they lowered it into water and weighed it again. Look at the pictures and complete the table.

	Weight in ________
weight of stone in air	________
weight of stone ________	________
upthrust of water	________

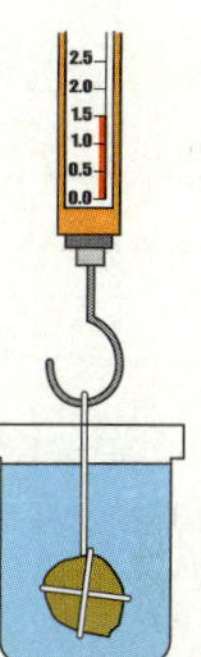

4 What force causes the spring in the forcemeter to stretch? ________________

Task 6 Gravity and Earth

Connor and Michael live in opposite parts of the Earth.

1 What keeps them both on the surface of the Earth? ________________

2 Each of them has a helium-filled balloon. On the diagram, show the direction of the force of gravity on the two balloons.

3 What is the force of gravity doing to their balloons?

____

Task 7 Parachutes

1 Parachutes are designed to fall slowly through the air. On the drawing of the parachute, use arrows to show the sizes and directions of the force of gravity and the force of air resistance. The length of the arrow represents the size of the force.

Some children did an investigation to find out if the area of the canopy of a parachute affected the time it took to reach the ground. They made their parachutes from the same material and always dropped them from the same height in the school hall.

2 Was this a fair test? Why?

____

Here are their results:

	Time to fall to ground (seconds)			
Area of canopy (cm^2)	1st go	2nd go	3rd go	mean
200	2.0	3.0	2.5	
400	4.0	4.5	3.5	
800	6.5	7.0	6.5	
1200	10.0	11.0	9.0	

3 Calculate the mean time for each parachute.

4 Why did they test each parachute three times?

____

5 Use the grid below to draw a graph of the results. Put the area of the canopy on the horizontal axis and the time to fall to the ground on the vertical axis. Remember to give the graph a title, and to use a ruler.